"Dr. Marcus Small has written an important work for couples who are married, for couples who are newlyweds, and for couples who are considering marriage. The title of the book suggests that only African American couples will benefit from his insights and his inspiration. Nothing could be further from the truth.

Although the suggestions are written from the context of the experience of Africans living in America, the helpful hints, the action-guide suggestions, and the questions for conversation can be used by couples of every ethnicity.

This work is not only one of those 'must-read' books for clergy, marriage counselors, pre-marital therapists, and persons in the helping professions, but it is also one of those 'books I have been waiting for!' volumes. It is a book about which many married couples will say, 'Where were you when I needed you?' when they open its pages and are blessed by the divine insights given by God to Dr. Small who is both a pastor and a scholar.

All couples, whether considering marriage, newlyweds, or 'seasoned saints,' will benefit from the present-tense participle 'becoming,' which is not only in the title of this work but is also the focus of each chapter. The Hebrew Scriptures say that 'A man is to leave his father and mother and cleave unto his wife and the two shall *become* one flesh.' Becoming suggests a process.

The journey of marriage is not a finished product when the pastor, the priest, the rabbi, or the Imam pronounces the couple husband and wife at the altar. The journey of marriage is an ongoing process, which the word 'becoming' suggests.

I recommend this work to you and guarantee you that God will bless your life as new insights are opened up to you in each chapter. This book is truly a page-turner. Enjoy the journey!"

— Jeremiah A. Wright Jr., pastor emeritus,
Trinity United Church of Christ, Chicago

"*Becoming Married, Staying Married* clearly and concisely presents an exploration of the realities, myths, and assumptions of marriage through pastoral theology, historical interrogation, ministerial marriage counseling, and personal experience. The scenarios, discussion questions, and action steps in each provocative chapter provide the perfect counter to vapid, contemporary, ghost-written self-help books; preponderance of negative-only marriage experiences; reality-show fodder; soap-opera storylines; and celebrity-based marriage-advice shows. This book is a must-read for those contemplating marriage or marriage counseling, active clergy, and seminary students."

— Teresa L. Fry Brown, Bandy Professor of Preaching,
Candler School of Theology, Emory University,
and Executive Director of Research and Scholarship,
African Methodist Episcopal Church

"The institution of marriage was birthed and ordained by the Creator as the foundational expression of the relational character of creation. The human is not designed to be alone, and the most revealing and authentic embodiment of togetherness is a genuine marriage. If marriage is purposed to model the intent and design of the Eternal, we can expect that inimical forces and powers will make every effort to injure and diminish the gift of this union. We desperately need resources that help us claim, heal, and restore the power and promise of marriage. Dr. Small has come to the rescue and penned a powerful and practical resource that dispels ignorance and exposes destructive behaviors that lead to the dissolution of the two who have become one. His thoughtful analysis, wise counsel, and practical suggestions inform, equip, and inspire all who seek to become married.

'What God has joined together, let no man or woman put asunder.'"

— John W. Kinney, Samuel DeWitt Proctor
School of Theology, Virginia Union University

"There are not enough thoughtful books on African American marriage. Marcus Small has aptly framed the discussion of marriage, first becoming and then staying. Many people want the happiness of a beautiful wedding ceremony without the work required for the joys of marriage. Pastor Small brings his keen insight, pastoral hope, and unique wit to this subject matter that is both challenging and engaging at the same time. I cannot wait to use this helpful tool for couples considering the call to matrimony and the journey to marriage."

— Gary V. Simpson, pastor, The Concord Baptist Church
of Christ, Brooklyn, and Associate Professor of Homiletics,
Drew University Theological School

Becoming Married, Staying Married

Becoming Married, Staying Married

A Guide for African American Couples

Marcus Small

WESTMINSTER
JOHN KNOX PRESS
LOUISVILLE • KENTUCKY

First edition
Published by Westminster John Knox Press
Louisville, Kentucky

17 18 19 20 21 22 23 24 25 26—10 9 8 7 6 5 4 3 2 1

Book design by Drew Stevens
Cover design by designpointinc.com

Library of Congress Cataloging-in-Publication Data

Names: Small, Marcus, author.
Title: Becoming married, staying married : a guide for African American couples / Marcus Small.
Description: Louisville, KY, : Westminster John Knox Press, 2017. | Includes bibliographical references.
Identifiers: LCCN 2017023310 (print) | LCCN 2017032389 (ebook) | ISBN 9781611648355 (ebk.) | ISBN 9780664262952 (pbk. : alk. paper)
Subjects: LCSH: Marriage—Religious aspects—Christianity. | African Americans—Religious life.
Classification: LCC BV835 (ebook) | LCC BV835 .S55115 2017 (print) | DDC 248.8/4408996073—dc23
LC record available at https://lccn.loc.gov/2017023310

Most Westminster John Knox Press books are available at special quantity discounts when purchased in bulk by corporations, organizations, and special-interest groups. For more information, please e-mail SpecialSales@wjkbooks.com.

To the ancestors who struggled so we would have
the opportunity to become even greater
and
To Cassandra, for twenty years of becoming us

Contents

Foreword

"We learn about love in childhood."

—Bell Hooks

Scholar/activist bell hooks offers a simple meditation on love in the above statement. It is a statement fraught with a complicated history and enormous consequences. Love is an overused term and an undervalued virtue. America, in particular, has sought to co-opt the term "love" for promotion and market-driven production while simultaneously exorcising the difficult, rough, demanding aspects of "love" from the discussion. Love becomes, in this manifestation, an object to be obtained, a product to be bought, or a physical idea to be touched; but it is rarely a spiritual value to be lived. A consequence of our societal allergic reaction to love is that we are witnessing increased marriages steeped in turmoil. The work of love is missed and the ill-fated romantic notion of mysterious love is embraced. As a result, couples climb into the boat of marriage without sails, forced to survive against the natural and tumultuous currents of life. One could take this metaphor further and claim marriages are in trouble, not because couples do not share love, but because they have become seasick and unable to navigate the currents of marital existence.

The role of the preacher is to proclaim good news to the vulnerable and counsel the broken. Couples caught by the gale-force winds of living need a guiding voice and hand. Pastor Marcus Small has created such a book. I would daresay this book is a lighthouse, beckoning ships lost just a few feet beyond the horizon, to come safely to shore. In every congregation, marital questions and conflict bustle around the altar. Men and women of faith, and love, attempt to make sense of the world through the lens of faith. Unfortunately, many pastors are not equipped to deal with such inquiry. The book you hold in your hand is the resource we've been praying for. With humor, insight, and theological depth, Pastor Marcus (as he is affectionately called by millennial parishioners) provides ministers, lay leaders, and couples with a framework to build healthy relationships and the tools to banish destructive habits. This is the book our community has been searching for, and I am proud to say a good friend, who is an excellent preacher and master teacher, was given the assignment to create such a resource. I pray that this publication will enrich your life and find a permanent place on your shelf and that you will come to know why "Pastor Marcus" is a shining theological light, called to burn brightly in this age of doubt and, at times, despair.

Otis Moss III
Chicago, Illinois
2017

Acknowledgments

The process of getting a book together is an act of becoming all its own. There are so many pieces working together at the same time that it can sometimes be hard to keep up. I am grateful to many for helping this project come together. I am thankful to my dear friend Reverend Dr. Otis Moss III for encouraging me to write these ideas down and for his assistance with the foreword. I would like to thank Brother David Maxwell from Westminster John Knox Press for his guidance and his patience with me through this process. Thank you to the wonderful people at WJK for their professionalism and warm spirits of cooperation. To Michelle E. Shaw for her outstanding gifts and skills and her great eye for detail. To Reverend Dr. Gina M. Stewart and Reverend Dr. Lester A. McCorn for giving a thumbs up to the project, I am grateful to you as well.

I would like to thank all of the people in the churches that nurtured my growth and development. To my home church, the New Hope Baptist Church of Hackensack, New Jersey, and the church that licensed and ordained me, The Imani Baptist Church of Christ of East Orange, New Jersey. I am grateful for the examples that were given to me by the wonderful people who showed me what the love of God and of extended family looks like. To them I am eternally grateful. I am grateful to the members, leadership, and churches that I have been blessed to serve in the capacity of minister: Salem Baptist Church of Jersey City, New Jersey, Ebenezer Baptist Church of Englewood, New Jersey, and New Calvary Baptist Church of Norfolk, Virginia. It is in these places of worship where people have trusted me with their feelings and their relationships, and they have helped me formulate these thoughts about marriage that are in this work. I thank them for their trust in me, and I pray that I have been responsible to them in the guidance and information I have tried to lovingly share over the years.

I would like to thank all my mentors in ministry who have helped me grow—there are simply too many to name—people like my childhood pastor, Moses A. Knott Jr. and Reverend Dr. Gary V. Simpson, who I call my pastor. Dr. Jeremiah A. Wright Jr., Dr. James Perkins, Dr. John W. Kinney, Dr. Patricia Gould-Champ, Reverend Gregory J. Jackson, Dr. M. Frances Manning, Reverend Benjamin Whipper, Dr Teresa Fry-Brown, and Reverend D. Keith Owens. In one way or another they are a part of this project through their influences, words of wisdom and correction, and most of all their love, which has been a constant blessing to me. I have been honored to acquire the lessons as I have sat at their feet.

I would like to thank Reverend Martin Phillips LPC for being a great mentor in the field of counseling and reviewing the book. Thank you to the colleagues of Tidewater Pastoral Counseling Services in Norfolk for their support and prayers. To personal friends in ministry, I am grateful for your words of encouragement and most of all your laughter as you have allowed me to be me. To my friends, Dr. Reginald Williams Jr. and Dr. Eugene L. Gibson Jr., affectionately known as the Wolfpack, there are no words to express my love and appreciation.

Finally, to my family, to my grandparents Earnest and Rachel Brown, for still showing what love looks like for over sixty years. To William and Lucille Small Sr., for stressing the importance of building a legacy, to my parents William Small Jr. and Carolyn Brown, for not giving up on me and proving that prayer works. To my brothers Michael and Craig, you are my real heroes. To all my aunts and cousins and nieces and nephews, for their prayers and encouragement, and to my friends and the people who have crossed the path of my life. It is all in here. To my wife, Cassandra, who has with patience loved me for over twenty years, and to my daughter, Taylor, and son, Malcolm, thank you for letting me be a "busy daddy."

Most of all to the angel that walks with me, to God be the glory, let all the mistakes be mine.

Marcus Small
2017

Introduction

A young woman came into my office, wide-eyed, excited, and full of joy and self-confident assurance. "Pastor, it's happened! God has sent me the one I'm going to marry!" She was looking right at me, but held a long, far-off gaze full of love-struck emotion, mixed in with a look of "I hope he doesn't think I've lost it." She continued, "I asked God to send me someone. I told the Lord I would stop fighting and just open myself to God's will, and whoever the Lord chose to send me that's who God wants me to be with. When Reggie came into my life I knew he was the one!"

Is this you? Have you found "the one"? Or, if you've been married for a while, do you remember this feeling?

One of the joys of being a pastor is witnessing this moment in peoples' lives. Women and men come to see me, filled with the elation of the recent proposal and the joy of a mutual decision to marry. They seem so happy and so sure.

But the looks on their faces often change to concern when I ask them to schedule an appointment with their fiancé so that they can begin their premarital counseling. Almost immediately, it's like I've told them a family member has died. They

1

look at me with such disappointment: "Really, Pastor, do you think that's necessary? I mean I just told you this is the work of the Lord. I see God's hand in this . . . God has *sent* him to me! We just need to plan the wedding!"

This is where the work of marriage begins for many couples. The truth is that couples deciding to get married need to prepare themselves as much as possible for the life journey they will share together. Some couples are hesitant and comply only to satisfy my requirement in order to perform their wedding. But many welcome the chance to begin to explore together what this journey might entail.

If you are reading this book, it is because you want to explore what it means to become married, a process that only begins with the wedding ceremony. And if this book has been thrust into your hands by your fiancé, friend, or pastor, and you've been told you must read it, well, I hope you'll agree with me soon about how important this conversation is for you and your marriage.

Let's be real. People get married for all kinds of reasons. One of those reasons may be to escape a past that they are all too eager to forget. Counseling may bring up issues someone is trying to forget or hide from a future spouse. Maybe she won't want to get married to you if she knows these things.

It is a risk. But I'm convinced it is a risk couples must take if they want to create a healthy, long-lasting relationship. Believe me, your spouse also has issues. And you do not need to share absolutely everything with your spouse. But if you both can trust each other and commit to this process of becoming married, I assure you that you will also become more comfortable with yourselves and better individuals.

THE ROLLER COASTER OF MARRIAGE

I love roller coasters, the bigger the better. There is something about looking at that mountain of twists and turns while standing in line with anticipation. People get on and return with looks of excitement and adrenaline in their faces, and I can hardly contain myself knowing it will be the same with me. Once it's finally my turn, attendants help me into the ride and instruct me how to secure myself for the ride. Before they give the "OK" sign to start the ride, they come by and check to make sure that everyone is safe and secure. The attendant at the microphone shouts additional instructions—what to do with your hands, make sure you don't stand up, make sure you are in the seat at all times. No matter how ready I think I am, there are rules, regulations, and suggestions to help me have the best experience possible.

Couples who make the decision to get married feel the excitement and adrenaline rush that marriage brings. Enjoy that rush! Sure, your married friends can give you some advice on what it's like for them, but there are some things that you need to know before you get on the marriage roller coaster to ensure a better ride. If you don't know what to expect, you may want to get off before you even get started. This book is for couples who want to prepare themselves in order to have a good ride.

MARRIAGE IS MORE THAN ROMANCE

The main reason couples jump onto the marriage rollercoaster without buckling their seatbelts is because they are overwhelmed with all the love they are feeling. Love, in its simplest form, is seen as the ultimate marriage fixer, the binder of all things difficult in relationships. Many couples believe this romantic love is the medicine that will keep them together through all situations, no matter how challenging or difficult things get.

I believe that love indeed can bind us together and that romance is a key element of married love. When we enter into the marriage covenant with one another, we have the opportunity to be servants of God in the truest understanding of ministry. Ministry is simply defined as service, and when we are married, we enter into service for each other. We not only offer ourselves to service, but we also partner with another individual to do service together. Our spouse becomes someone we share a life with and also the person we share our ministry and faith with. The things that are done as a couple, the lives that are touched, the possible children and other family members that are blessed by the couple are all done essentially through the ministry of marriage. Marriage is a covenant between two people who believe that God is in the process of creating something with their union. But to understand what God is up to, we need to understand how marriage works as individuals.

CHALLENGE YOUR ASSUMPTIONS

The first challenge for couples is to take a hard look at the ideas and perceptions they have about marriage. Our perceptions of marriage often have little to do with the person we're getting married to and have everything to do with what we want, what we've dreamed of, and what we've been taught, consciously and unconsciously, about marriage. It is a challenge to question preconceived notions and turn them into a beneficial process that develops a healthy and productive marriage. Part of this process is making sure that there is a healthy understanding not only of what marriage is, but also of what a marriage should *become.* As I will say countless times in this book, marriage is a process of becoming. It never ends.

As a couple getting married, or recently married, you probably are not thinking a lot about what your marriage will look like in ten, twenty, or thirty years. Sure, you may have thought about where you might live or what your children might look like should you choose and be able to have or adopt them. But few couples beginning their marriage journey see themselves years away from their wedding date and contemplate what their marriage will become.

— How will you solve problems?
— How will you deal with trying situations—what happens when one of you gets laid off from work and you have only one income?

—How will you work through tough decisions about an annoying family member moving in and how long he will be allowed to stay? Or what if one of you gets promoted and is required to move and relocate to a different state?

—How might you make it through the death of a child, or parenting a child with special needs who needs lifelong care?

—How will you handle an infidelity if it occurs?

Many things happen for which no couple can prepare. Moments such as these bring tremendous stress to the relationship. Life will test your marriage in some very real ways: the love you feel can get tested, the fears you had can become realities, and what you once thought God brought together can be questioned with great frequency!

In case this is sounding too depressing, there is hope! Couples who have faced these challenges and countless others have managed to weather those storms and continue the process of becoming a couple. If the process is done right, couples learn not only more about each other, but also how to navigate through tough times together. They *become* a couple on a deeper level.

WHAT'S YOUR COUPLE PERSONALITY?

As they go through life together, couples develop a certain kind of personality, a fingerprint, that becomes distinctly theirs. In the movies *Why Did I Get Married?* and *Why Did I Get Married Too?* we find couples who show their couple personalities. Patricia and Gavin initially were the "lovey-dovey" couple who talked and shared everything, even when things got difficult. Terry and Diane were the "true professionals" who worked hard on making their way up the corporate success ladder. Mike and Sheila were the "disconnected couple" who never seemed to understand one another. And Marcus and Angela were the "fighting couple" who expressed themselves through conflict and tension.

Obviously, these couples are anything but perfect in their personalities. But they show that couples *become* something more than they are as individuals. Some couples who have been together forever still hug and kiss all over each other in public, making us nauseous with all their affections. We know couples that seem career driven and have a business-style approach to life, but somehow it works for them. There are couples who love to travel together and are always on the road. And, of course, there are those couples who seem to always be fighting and disagreeing about something. You hate to go out with them because you know they are going to embarrass you at the restaurant, but no matter how much they fuss, and no matter how much they argue, you know in the back of your mind neither of them is going anywhere.

What is your couple personality? Does it match your expectations of what you want it to be? Some couples feel defeated and deflated when their marriage doesn't look like what they imagined and they can feel that something is wrong. It might be. Or it might be that as a couple you offer a distinct personality that is a little different than both of you as individuals. The purpose of this book is to help you dialogue with your partner and begin a lifelong conversation so that you learn not only what it means to be married, but how to *become* married.

WHAT IS PREMARITAL/MARRIAGE COUNSELING?

Premarital counseling is simply some guided space given to a couple for them to achieve their particular goal of building a healthy marriage. "Good" counseling methods today are based on scientific research data, psychological information, and family history to properly assess and understand individuals' behavior patterns. Premarital counseling should help you first understand yourselves as individuals, and what you each bring to the relationship, and then to recognize how your gifts and baggage will be combined with what your partner brings. A dialogue then begins when you talk together about how you can navigate through those issues, assumptions, predictions, and expectations so that as individuals and as a couple you become better. Learning different techniques of communication, conflict resolution, and understanding of quality couple time all become methods in understanding what will be required of each of you to continue to develop a healthy marriage relationship.

Unfortunately, in our culture and especially in the African American community, a common understanding is that counseling is a sign of failure. If one sees a counselor, obviously there is a problem. While that can sometimes be the case, counseling is about getting clarity. We can get so caught up in the way we see things that we do not recognize other perspectives, ideas, approaches, and opinions. Premarital counseling helps couples, through the assistance of an objective party, broaden perspectives and learn how to improve the couple's connection and intimacy. Sometimes hearing a different perspective can help clear a clouded mind and open couples to ways of compromise that might not otherwise be seen.

Fortunately, a growing number of African Americans are discovering the benefits of counseling and therapy as assets to our communities. Historically, many understood that the church was the place where you took your troubles and you "turned them over to Jesus." This is certainly true, but the Lord has prepared some people to give us some helpful, outside guidance. In fact, the Greek word *Paraclete*, the word that we use for the "Holy Spirit," actually means "advocate" or "helper." The counselor serves as an instrument of the Holy Spirit to help guide, encourage, and console those who find themselves in situations where they need clarity.

WHY A BOOK FOR AFRICAN AMERICAN COUPLES?

Simply put, our community needs to help those who choose to be married so that their marriages are stronger and our community is strengthened. While marriage rates in the U.S. have plummeted in recent years, in 2011 fifty-five percent of whites were married, compared with thirty-one percent of African Americans.[1] This is alarming. When we look at marriage and what it means to the development and health not only of individuals but of a community as well, we have to wonder why our community is less coupled or able to sustain marriages than other communities.

This rapid decline in marriage has transformed how African Americans see family and how we see community. Our childrearing alone has changed with the decline of marriage as more households are becoming single parent homes. The U.S. Census reported that 52.1 percent of African American children were living in single parent homes. Without a doubt, children can grow and develop healthily in a single parent home, but the question must be asked: Why is that becoming the norm more than the exception?

In chapter 4 we will discuss the history of marriage in the African American community more in detail, but for now, I want to say that I believe that healthy, strong marriages can be good examples for the African American community. As was stated earlier, marriages aren't just for the individuals. Your marriage can serve as a ministry for the community. Spending time together before you get married to discuss how you will communicate, what you expect, and other matters can set you on the path to becoming married.

HOW TO USE THIS BOOK

Part 1 of this book consists of five chapters about marriage in general. We will look at some assumptions about marriage and where those assumptions come from, how marriage might be seen as a ministry, what individuals each bring to a marriage, marriage in the African American community and how it is different, and what a healthy relationship looks like.

Part 2 of this book will examine what I call "becoming qualities" that will help any marriage remain healthy. We will look at these qualities as useful tools for good marriages. The qualities include having a good sense of self-awareness, effectively communicating, resolving conflict, learning the act of forgiveness, learning how to be flexible, learning the meaning of "marriage mature," and expressing sexuality in a healthy way.

Each chapter ends with some questions for you to think about and hopefully discuss as a couple. And some suggested actions steps are also provided for you to consider.

Although this book speaks to both pre-marriage and recently married couples, the fact is that all couples can learn and refresh from these techniques and perspectives at any time in their relationship. Also, while written with African American couples in mind, most of the book is totally applicable for any marriage. For couples where just one of the spouses is African American, the information about particularities of African Americans and marriage will be especially helpful to discuss.

My prayer is that this book will open the door for you and your fiancé to have a conversation about your hopes and expectations of what you desire to become. The true success of all relationships is connection, and we who are in relationship need to work on those connections on a daily basis. I pray you experience joy on this journey of becoming. It can be a lovely ride.

PART ONE

Becoming Married

1

Becoming Aware

Fairy Tales and the Realities of Marriage

The same mouth that courts you doesn't marry you.
—Caribbean Proverb

When morning came, there was Leah! So Jacob said to Laban,
"What is this you have done to me? I served you for Rachel,
didn't I? Why have you deceived me?"
—Genesis 29:25

Did you ever dream about getting married? You probably
imagined who you'd marry, how amazing that person would
be, and the sort of life the two of you would have. Many people make up stories, fairy tales even, about their future lives.
But, as Anita Baker sings, "The story ends, as stories do, reality steps into view."[1]

When it comes to relationships, it is hard not to create fairy
tales. You have grandiose ideas about what kinds of places you
will live, what kinds of trips and vacations you will take, how
many kids you will have, and what they will look like. Such
dreams are pleasant to have and quite common during the dating portion of relationships. The dream becomes a sort of test-
ing ground for the kind of spouse you desire. You have real
conversations about the fantasy to find out what you have in
common, if you have the same types of values, and if your
life goals and objectives match on any level. This process can
help couples come together and generate excitement about the
future. But in the imaginary phase, you often miss important
traits of the real people in the relationship.

Reality is distorted within the fairy tale because your conversations focus on the fantasy. If your conversations rarely deal with the reality of who you both are, you never really talk about what bothers you or what you like and what you don't like. You don't discuss your real hang-ups and the ugly things you know about yourself. It is often in the moments after the "I dos" when Anita Baker appears prophetic and "reality steps into view," that you realize that you haven't talked about who you really are as an individual, what you are looking for out of life, and what you expect out of this marriage. The fairy tale begins to fade and you are faced with an unknown and uncomfortable reality.

Reality stepped into view for Kevin and Audrey, a young couple in my church, and they came to see me. While there are multiple things that contribute to Audrey's and Kevin's storyline, the three that this chapter will highlight are: unspoken expectations, personal ambassadors, and media influences. Unspoken expectations can be dangerous in a dating relationship and marriage. You make room for these intruders when you don't speak up about things that you desire, think, and feel. One of the reasons you keep things to yourself is because you want your beloved to see the best parts of you. You put that portion of yourself on display, and that partial personality becomes your personal ambassador, of sorts. That ambassador is constructed from a variety of beliefs, including what you've learned from friends, family, and the church; but there are also influences from television and film, which is the last thing discussed in this chapter.

UNSPOKEN EXPECTATIONS

About five months into Audrey and Kevin's marriage, they came to my office. The mood was tense; they smiled nervously through clinched teeth.

Pastor:　OK, so . . . why are we here today?

Audrey:　He has not kept any of his promises with this marriage!

Kevin: I can't win Rev. It's like every time I do something, it's not good enough. I try to listen to her. I try to work with her. But the more I try, the less she thinks I can do. It's wearing me out!

Pastor: What promises do you feel Kevin hasn't kept?

Audrey: (tearfully) He said he wouldn't neglect me, he said he would make me the number one priority, he said he wouldn't push me off for his boys.

Kevin: She wants me to be there every moment of the day, she wants me to get off work and come home and sit with her and talk. If I say I'm going to play ball with my friend, she gets an attitude and she says I don't care about her. And another thing, she's always talking about if I care about her I would give her flowers a few times a week or take her out to nice restaurants when we go out. C'mon Rev, do I look like I'm made of money?

Audrey: (crying) You didn't have a problem getting me flowers when you were trying to get me, but now it's too much of a problem. You certainly aren't who you pretended to be.

One of the issues that plague Kevin and Audrey's marriage is the dream they created during the dating portion of their relationship. They each expected the marriage to be an extension of their dating relationship. Audrey thought she would continue to get showered with flowers and have the same amount of Kevin's attention that she previously enjoyed. Kevin thought he could maintain his pre-marriage friendships and habits. But reality stepped into view for each of them. The flowers were getting expensive for Kevin and he bought them less often, and Audrey did not get the attention from her husband that she expected, which left her feeling deceived.

The truth of the matter is, you do not anticipate the changes that occur between dating and marriage. You have expectations that certain things will stay the same and your significant other will continue the same routines and patterns. Yet shifts in behavior and thought processes are part of the package. One of the struggles of a new marriage is the lack of conversation, between the couple, about their rational and realistic expectations of each other. You often assume that your partner knows what you want. They know what you want because they love you, right? They know what you want, not because you have told them, but because of osmosis. Yes, osmosis. You know, when your beloved does that one perfect thing, and you just know they "get" you, so you don't have to actually mention what you expect because they already know. But that is not how this works. Your partner may have gotten lucky with that perfect gesture, but when it does not happen again, you can begin to feel like you've been led on. This is where we find Audrey and Kevin, but they're not the only ones.

Jacob in the book of Genesis, gives us a similar story. He was an ambitious individual. He came out of his mother's womb clutching his brother Esau's heel; he was known for looking to get himself ahead. He fell in love with a woman named Rachel and agreed to work for seven years to earn her hand in marriage. According to the Bible, he was so in love with her that the time flew by. The wedding night finally came, and Jacob shared a bed with his new wife. But when he woke up the next morning, and lifted the veil from his bride's face, he found out he'd married Rachel's older sister, Leah. In this case, Jacob actually *had* married a different person, but the feeling of betrayal he felt still applies: He did not get the marriage he expected. Jacob likely felt that he had wasted seven years of his life.

How many of you would feel the same way, after working hard to nurture a relationship? You meet someone, you say everything you're supposed to say and do everything you think you're supposed to do. You are in love and can see marriage in the distance, so you work toward the goal of having that person tell you they want to be with only you. To make sure that happens, you don't mention the things you don't like or talk about things you don't enjoy.

You long for the moment when your beloved is completely yours. You've worked for it, invested in it, and you've even prayed for it. But many times, like Jacob, once the sun comes up and the veil is lifted, you realize that what you have is not what you expected. You don't construct these fairy tales to intentionally deceive; you create the fantasy because you're trying to put forth a good impression. You want to make sure that people see the best about you. You're careful with your thoughts, you don't say things that might offend, and you make plans that you usually wouldn't. Like master strategists, you create such a winning image it would be difficult for anyone to turn you down.

PERSONAL AMBASSADORS

Ambassadors are people appointed by a government to represent that government to other nations. Ambassadors go to a specific country to establish or maintain good relationships. Ambassadors make sure peace is established, they keep small infractions from becoming major problems, and they entertain and host guests who visit the country. An ambassador is essential in maintaining good relationships between two countries. The same sequence holds true in dating relationships. When you date someone seriously, you often send your ambassador self to represent you, and your partner does the same. That's right, you're not the only one with an ambassador—your beloved has one, too! The ambassadors work together, like ally countries. The images you create of yourself are not an intentional deception, but it is deceiving nonetheless because you never really know what is going on in your intended's home country. You only know what the ambassador shows you. There is no talk about the unrest in your lives, and each ambassador showcases only the best attributes. Your ambassador makes small talk of the issues that may really be big problems, because the goal is to keep your romantic interest . . . interested. Your ambassadors work hard, but what happens when you and your partner

realize what you've seen is not the whole story? There are pot-
holes in the streets, not all the buildings are up to code, and
there is a lot of work to be done. What happens after you suc-
cessfully convince your beloved's country to partner with your
country of love, but you both have to live with the hidden, ugly
realities that you did not see at first?

Relationship psychotherapist John Karter says, "Most of us
are so focused on what we expect to get, based on romantic
ideals, cultural norms and media propaganda, that the qualities, standards, values and emotional input we actually need to
be happy and fulfilled within a relationship are ignored."[2] You
want to believe certain things about the people you date, just
like you want them to believe certain things about you, even if
the information isn't entirely accurate. You work hard to get
people to like you and approve of you, so you often neglect to
show your true selves. You want to feel accepted and be reas-
sured that your feelings or affection will be returned, which is
one of the reasons you share carefully curated images of yourself. You want to impress the people who mean something to
you, and when you think you've found someone who you may
want to share your life with, his opinion matters. But so much
effort to impress someone could lead to forgetting the "real"
you. You become accustomed to the ambassador, and the perfection that comes with it, on a constant basis. Karter believes
you work so hard on the fairy tale that the real things that
you need in a relationship are never really addressed. You look
for certain patterns and behaviors in a potential mate, but you
rarely connect or have a true intimate experience, thanks to the
work of the ambassador.

Your ambassadors encourage you to forget your authentic
selves. Oftentimes, you allow the ambassador to represent you
for so long, you begin to believe the "real" you will be far less
exciting. You don't want your love interest to see the insecurities
you carry, you don't want a potential mate to see the ugly habits
you've formed over the years, you don't want a possible life partner to realize how much you don't know, even after you've pretended to know so much. Instead, you find yourself walking into

marriages with some profound secrets, which only exist because you were too afraid to open yourself up to the one with whom you want to share the rest of your life. How ironic it is to want someone who will love you, even with your faults, but you are too afraid to talk about the existence of those faults. About these secrets, psychologist David L. Smith wrote, "Even in marriage, which your culture holds as the very paragon of intimacy and trust, you find that partners keep secrets from one another about money, past experiences (particularly sexual experiences), current flirtations, 'bad' habits, aspirations and worries, their children, real opinions about friends and relatives and so on."[3] But why do we keep these secrets? Here are a few reasons:

Fear – Sometimes we feel that if we share our true feelings and opinions that we will no longer be considered special or appreciated. Our desire to be considered an influence in someone's life can keep us from expressing what we think about certain issues.

Masking – In relationships, especially new ones, we tell ourselves that the habits or behaviors that bother us about the other person aren't a big deal. We convince ourselves that we can ignore these problems, but that is not true.

Pressure – We often put pressure on our beloved to make changes in their own lives, changes that are tied to our fear and masking. This action is based on two false assumptions: that our partner knows what needs to be changed, and that the thing that offends us is also seen as a problem for them.

Love – Known as the great equalizer, it is thought that love will conquer all. We believe that if we love someone enough, and if someone loves us enough, we can look past certain relationship problems. The fact is, however, the things that annoy us will never go away and will inevitably create problems later.

These are just a few examples of why we don't really reveal our true selves. We are fearful of being honest and so we hold in things that our partners really need to know, and we can end up creating a deeper rift than getting closer to one another.

In your relationships, you are called to understand each other on a level that is often uncomfortable to access. You should feel comfortable opening yourself up to your beloved, and you should feel safe doing so. This is the meaning of true intimacy: communicating on such an intimate level that you can be honest with each other about your anxieties, dreams, hopes, and ambitions.

You hold on to the masks that you wear because of your own anxieties, not the fears of others. You hold things back in relationships because you are afraid of others getting too close or that others will figure out who you really are inside. You are also afraid of being controlled and told what to do or being abandoned. As long as you continue to play chess with your feelings, these issues will not be resolved. You must establish a true intimate connection with your mate, because she will cherish you and protect your deepest fears. Your beloved will not carry, or take on, your fears for you, but she will extend the love and grace of God to help you discover ways you can grow past the fairy tale.

MEDIA INFLUENCE

I enjoy a good love story. My romantic side allows me to root for the underdog and cheer for love. You know the stories: the unpopular guy gets the girl of his dreams; the girl who didn't get asked to the prom leaves with the most popular boy in school. These are great stories. We all cheer for the person who is seemingly unable to find love but somehow manages to find their way into the arms of someone who truly loves them. We all would love to be swept off of our feet and have that one person tell us that he will love us like no one else in the world. Maybe that happened for you. But in life, unlike after the credits roll, there is more to the tale. We have to work to keep our love story alive. We have a responsibility to write our own script after the movie is over.

A more negative portrayal of marriage is also spread by Hollywood. For years, television has made the contentious marriage a norm in family sitcoms. An example of this was the show called *The Honeymooners*, with Ralph Kramden promising his wife, Alice, that one day with a "bang, zoom" he would send her to the moon. Years ago, on the television show *All in the Family*, Archie Bunker bickered with his wife, Edith, the "dingbat," as he constantly referred to her. Not to be outdone, the African American spinoff show, *The Jeffersons*, always had George Jefferson, the hot-headed dry cleaners tycoon, in heated arguments with his wife, Louise; the two continuously exchanged insults in their deluxe apartment in the sky. The perception of dysfunction and marriage made its way into the psyche of those who watched these shows under the guise of slap-stick comedy and entertainment.

The images of marriage and relationships on television and film have helped support the image of marriage being a burden or something that can be figured out with a quick decision and a warm fuzzy feeling. The cable channels draw attention to the made-up scenarios of married life. But do we really want to take our relationship cues from the shows we watch?

I like to play chess, especially with my son. I think something about the process of anticipating the next move excites him. He loves to try and figure out my next move. His entire strategy is based on what he thinks I will do next. This is how some relationships function, when we make moves that respond to our partner's actions. When you let ambassadors, fairy tales, and fantasies into your marriage, you will find yourself playing chess on a regular basis. When you hold on to things, or you don't share how you truly feel, you are planning your next move on the chessboard. You wait to see what your partner does before you make a move, but more than that, you try to figure out what they will do so you can anticipate what is going to happen next. When you play chess with your feelings and emotions, you turn your relationship into a game, and when you play games in marriage, no one ever wins.

Marriage is about working through the images and ideas of your imaginations and dreams. You must be willing to understand that the ideas you bring into a relationship are just pieces of the puzzle and that your spouse has her own ideas of marriage as well. The reality of marriage then is created by the couple, who must figure out what it will take to enjoy life beyond the fairy tale.

Questions to Discuss Together

1. What fairy tales exist in your relationship that need to be examined?
2. Name one unspoken expectation each of you have of one another. After you name that expectation, allow the other person to respond. Is it real? Is it something he can do? How would she alter it?
3. How have media portrayals of marriage, good and bad, influenced your expectations of a "good" marriage?

Action Step

Hold a meeting between your ambassador selves. Tell the other person's ambassador just how great your individual self is. Then tell the person something you may have stretched a little just to impress them.

NOTES

2
Becoming Knowledgeable
Understanding How the Two Shall Become One

To get lost is to learn the way.

—African Proverb

That is why a man leaves his father and mother and is united to his wife, and they become one flesh.

—Genesis 2:24

In the initial stages of courtship, when we have those thoughts that the person may indeed be "the one," it is often because we feel safe and trust our intended spouse. We feel like we can share and experience certain things with our beloved, and we expect our beloved feels the same about us. We share all kinds of experiences and events both past and present with our partners and build a sense of trust and openness.

We continue this process of sharing through the courtship, the engagement, and even up to the wedding event, but something happens after the wedding that causes us to somehow or another stop sharing. We assume that we have shared all that there is about us and there is nothing left to say, or if our spouse truly wants to know something about us, they will ask. We don't find it necessary to share the experiences of the day and find ourselves moving into our own corners. Roles and responsibilities are broken up and the assignments of who needs to do what are passed out. What slowly begins to happen under this false sense of working together is that we find ourselves as couples with little to talk about and even fewer common interests. Time goes by and days are spent checking lists and running kids to soccer and music recitals, and little time is given to the investment of what is needed as a couple. So we find ourselves either continuing in that pattern and simply tolerating each other, or we make plans for divorce or separation because we feel we have nothing in common.

The reality is that every relationship must continue in the path of growing and developing. Couples see their responsibility as parents, breadwinners, schedule keepers, and bill payers, when the truth is the foundation of all that is done happens as a connected married couple. The marriage commitment should always be a priority for couples because it is that commitment that will not only strengthen you as a couple but will also help strengthen your relationship in the challenging moments of your lives. When challenges enter into a relationship, the stress level that is created can be so trying that marriages begin to come apart and unravel. The work and time invested in the relationship before reaching those moments of challenge can help marriages endure the moments of vulnerability. This ability to endure and work together is a part of the development process. This quality doesn't just happen. It must be developed over the course of time. The reason why many divorces happen early in marriage is because couples are not willing to or do not know how to endure the challenges they face as a couple, and much of that has to do with the time and investment we all must make in our marriages and our spouses.

Jade and Alex had been married for about five years when they came to talk about their marriage and what they could do about it.

> **Pastor:** So, why are we here today?
>
> **Alex:** We're trying to find out where our marriage went wrong.
>
> **Pastor:** Why do you feel it has gone wrong?
>
> **Alex:** It just seems like I'm living with a stranger, it seems like we're roommates, not like we're a couple.

Jade: Don't get us wrong, we love each other, we just don't know why we don't *like* each other.

Pastor: Well OK, tell me what you do with each other. Jade, what kind of things do you do together?

Jade: We don't do much, just sleep because we're always working. I just got a new job and Alex works alternate shifts so his hours change and now he's working nights, so we barely see each other.

Alex: And there's the baby, it seems that everything is about the baby. Doctor's appointments, talking about who is picking him up and who's dropping him off, who's turn is it to change him and who's supposed to put him to bed and feed him. Don't get me wrong, I love my son, but it seems like that's all we do!

What Alex and Jade are experiencing is not uncommon, but it is also not terribly healthy. Many couples go through adjustments when jobs change or children come into play, and the time for getting used to the change can be a difficult one, but the one thing that must remain is the contact that you have growing and investing in your spouse. A rule of thumb for couples is that when you notice that it's hard to find time for your spouse, that is a clear indication that you need to work harder to find time for your spouse! Make the time to invest in your partner—that time will be what gives you the strength to make it through your challenging times. Jade and Alex are so busy focusing on things outside of their relationship that they are no longer growing as a couple.

All things need to develop, all things need a process in which they grow and evolve over time. We understand this process when it comes to growing plants, but it also applies to relationships. Don't assume your relationships will grow because you love each other, or simply because you took the vows at the altar to be married. At the altar, you make a covenant to commit yourselves to becoming a married couple. The courtship and engagement period are important, but you are not finished growing as a couple. Women and men must learn how to be married because they should discover what will work for them as a couple. The process of becoming married is not gender specific. There is not one person or gender who has a better sense or instinct about how to develop as a couple.

Many couples, like Jade and Alex, drift apart as time passes. We work on careers, we take care of family members, and before you know it we've found out we have less and less to say to each other. Drifting apart contributes to the process of unbecoming a married couple. The process of drifting apart can happen the minute we convince ourselves that we can put off doing something about our relationship. Often, we never get around to doing anything until too much time has passed. While it may take a long time to reach a crisis point, rebuilding relationships doesn't happen overnight either.

In Genesis 2, God creates humanity in God's image, and God gives Adam the responsibility of naming those things that God has created. Although Adam has the responsibility of naming all the creatures, there is nothing that Adam can connect with on an intimate level. Adam is the only creature of his kind, and so although Adam is a steward of God's creation, he has no one to share his life with. God's purpose for creating Eve was that Adam might have a companion on the journey of life: "That is why a man leaves his father and mother and is united to his wife, and they become one flesh" (Gen. 2:24). What we often glance over when we read that text is the word "become." When a couple comes together to make a covenant with each other before God, they promise to engage in the process of living as a married couple. They are just starting the becoming process. The events that they will encounter as a couple will shape and further develop their relationship.

When people join a club or organization, there are expectations of members. Marriage must be looked at in the same way. It is not a commitment that stops being worked on after the ceremony and ritual of a wedding ceremony. The work of marriage must continue to move forward for the life of the relationship.

The relationships we commit ourselves to are supposed to offer many things, but one of the essential things that relationships should foster is a sense of companionship. That is why many couples can live in the same homes and raise children but not feel connected because the routine of marriage doesn't make them feel like they have companionship. To that same point, many people who are in unhappy marriages stay because they are afraid of being alone and believe that even a person who doesn't spend time with them or invest themselves with them is still a type of companion. But true connection is when you feel like you have a partner working with you, not just in the routine of the day, but building a life together.

HOW DO WE BECOME COUPLES?

In life, there is a process to becoming anything. Everything that you will ever do as an individual will require some kind of process to achieve it. Learning is a process. Learning to walk, ride a bike, and work the cash register are all processes. It doesn't matter what you want to become—a teacher, minister, doctor, engineer, or hip-hop dancer—the process of becoming requires two things: *learning* and *time*. If we want to understand something it will require that we learn about it. When we enter into a relationship with another, we make a commitment to grow with them through life's experiences. Marriage requires that we not only learn about each other as individuals but also learn what works for us as a couple. The rules and agreements that work for one couple may not work for another, simply because the personalities, views, and perspectives differ for each couple. The great challenge of all newly married couples is that they must learn about each other and what it means to be married. Becoming is a continuous process. Different things will come into your life as a couple, and with each event you will have to learn how to deal with the situation and how to work through the situation together as a couple. Even though some things may seem familiar, and there will be moments when you feel like you have been there before, they will still require something different from you and your spouse. When you stop learning you will stop growing together.

The other important factor for couples learning to become one is time. Time is a close cousin to learning in marriage. You need time to fully understand your spouse and the kind of couple you will become. Over time you will discover a pattern to how you make decisions, how you handle conflict, and how you make plans for the future. Those patterns need to be tweaked based on the situation at hand. New couples can find themselves frustrated if they don't set aside time to work on "becoming one." Your most beneficial asset in marriage will be patience. You will quickly learn that things will not go according to your schedule, but they will only happen when you work with your partner as a couple to achieve your marriage goals.

Time will help you understand your marital priorities. You will not waste time on things that do not matter, but you will automatically focus on the more important tasks as a couple. Time will help each of you understand the individual perspectives and approaches of your spouse in certain situations. It is important not to assume that you understand your partner too quickly or can determine what he is thinking. Always make sure that your partner feels included in the process of whatever is taking place. Give one another time to understand what it means to be a couple, and continue to give each other the space and opportunity to become a better partner.

MAKING MARRIAGE A PRIORITY

The path of becoming is important because individuals often find themselves feeling alone in their relationship. Like Alex and Jade in the beginning of this chapter, their issue was not a lack of love or concern, their issue was the absence of *feeling* love or concern. The challenge of many couples is to make the time to help your partner feel like they are a priority. If you were playing tennis with someone, and after a while they simply stopped running after the ball, they didn't hit the ball back to you, when you served it they just let the ball pass them, it would not take very long before you were tired of playing with them. The fact that they did not want to participate did not make the experience enjoyable and would lead you to believe that they didn't care or were simply uninterested.

Many times, a spouse might feel like she is in a game but is playing by herself. She feels like she does not have someone engaged in the process with her and begins to assume that her spouse doesn't care or is simply not interested. Now in the partner's case, that is not necessarily what he is actually feeling, but if there is no communication and dialogue of what is taking place, it leaves the frustrated spouse to wonder and assume it is how the partner feels. People in relationships need to feel connected; the companionship that comes from being together needs to be nurtured and cultivated on a regular basis. If it is not, people will find other interests and soon find themselves drifting apart.

John Gottman, author of *The Seven Principles for Making Marriage Work,* says couples should spend time putting money in each other's emotional bank accounts. He says through the conscious action of "turning toward" our partners, with small conversations and acknowledgments, we can actually stay connected and continue to grow as a couple. Investing in your spouse a little bit at a time helps to continue the continuity of the relationship and helps build an emotional reserve to pull from when the challenges of marriage appear.

Questions to Discuss Together

1. What expectations from your family history have you brought to your marriage? What about your marriage has surprised you the most?

2. What traits or characteristics have surprised you about your spouse? How have you adjusted in coming to terms with those discoveries?
3. What steps have you made to make your marriage a priority?

Action Step

Each person make a list of things you expect from your marriage. Share your list with your spouse and discuss which expectations are realistic and which are not.

NOTES

3

Becoming Honest

Discovering What We Bring to the Table

It is the habit that the child forms at home, that follows them to their marriage.

—Nigerian Proverb

For by the grace given me I say to every one of you: Do not think of yourself more highly than you ought, but rather think of yourself with sober judgment, in accordance with the faith God has distributed to each of you.

—Romans 12:3

Like it or not, we are intricately linked to our families of origin. Families of origin are simply the families that we come from, and we receive a lot from them. Biologically speaking, we get our features, our talents, our mannerisms, sometimes even our health issues from our families of origin. We can't help what we look like, how tall we are, how short we are, or how big our feet will be. Without the help of a plastic surgeon, we are stuck with what we get.

We are also connected to our families of origin in another way. In addition to our biological inheritance, we also inherit a behavioral and relationship DNA from our families. We learn from our families how to act, react, and conduct ourselves in our relationships. We learn, without even knowing it, how to deal with stress, how to treat problematic situations, how to deal with hostile people, how to confront problems, how to work with people, how to react to sad situations, how to get angry, and how to forgive. In essence, we learn how to function and operate in our marriages and relationships. We learn from our families of origin how to argue in relationships, how to resolve disputes, how to show affection, and how to communicate. We learn these things by watching the people operate in the relationships around us. "The family of origin, the family of birth, the family of creation, and the family of rearing are our first memberships in community, and the things learned in these early membership contexts become foundational for us."[1] As we develop our personalities, people of influence around us shape what we come to know and understand about how we connect with others and in our relationships.

Angela and Cooper made an urgent appointment with me. By the time they came in to see me, neither of them were speaking to each other. Upon asking them what the issue was, it was clear that Angela was more annoyed than Cooper. "He's not acting interested in anything, including me, and I am convinced that he doesn't care about this relationship!" she exclaimed. "Well, tell me why you think he doesn't care about you," I replied. She continued to elaborate: "He doesn't respond to me when I talk to him, he just sits there or doesn't say anything, and the more he stays quiet, the angrier I get." I looked at Cooper and try to get his reaction, "Cooper, do you shut down when Angela is talking to you, and if so, why do you think you do that?" He responded very assuredly: "First of all Rev, she doesn't talk, she *yells*! From sun up to sun down she's always yelling. Everything is an argument!" Angela quickly jumped in: "I'm not arguing, that's just the way I talk. Why don't you act like a man and stand up to me sometimes!" I watched Cooper's reaction and he was clearly frustrated by the insult but refused to say anything. "Cooper, you seem upset by what Angela said, do you think that was a fair assessment of who you are?" Cooper responded with a very controlled anger. "She does that to me all the time. She's always insulting me and trying to pick fights with me, but I promised my mother when I was growing up that I wouldn't fight with women." I asked him to explain what he meant. "When I was growing up my father would abuse my mother, and she would always tell me, 'When you get older don't ever hit or fight with women.' She told me that's not what real men do. So I'm trying not to get into any arguments." I look at Angela as the picture was becoming clearer to me. "Angela, do you understand why Cooper doesn't fight with you? He sees arguing as fighting with you, and in his mind he made a promise to his mom not to fight with women." Angela's feelings turned into criticism: "I don't understand why it's a problem, my parents would fight all the time, hit each other, punch each other, lock each other out of the house, that's what I see as fighting, we're not putting our hands on each other!"

Both Cooper and Angela's behaviors are working out of their families of origin. Cooper was taught that a man should never fight with a woman, and he interpreted arguing as a part of the fighting. Angela saw her parents fight each other even to the point of physical altercation, and she has learned that hostility is a part of the marriage relationship. So in Angela's mind, aggressive conflict shows that you care for each other, and in Cooper's mind, avoiding conflict is how you show care for one another. The harder Angela tries to get Cooper to respond, the more he retreats, even if it frustrates him to the point of anger. Both Cooper and Angela are operating from what they have learned from their families.

We need to understand, especially in our marriage relationships, that we have an unconscious loyalty to play out in our relationship models from our families of origin. The impact of that experience doesn't just affect us as children; that influence can last a lifetime. It is when we are in relationships and when we are connected to people outside of our family circle that we can begin to see behavioral patterns repeat themselves if we pay a little bit of attention. Of course, not everything we have learned from our families is bad, but some of us have learned hostility, criticism, holding secrets, avoiding conflict, negative thinking, being judgmental, and even verbal and physical abuse from our families. We don't automatically repeat everything that we've experienced in our family of origin; some experiences can cause us to do the opposite. We can take different approaches based on how we understand the behavior and what the behavior may have done to the family system. Understanding our families of origin means that we recognize where some of our behavior and thought patterns come from, and when we understand where we got our thinking and behavior, we can make conscious decisions to make the needed adjustments.

IT RUNS IN THE FAMILY

Remember the Bible story of Jacob? The one who was always working an angle, ambitious, and always looking to get ahead? That Jacob. One of the first things we learn about Jacob is he hustles his brother Esau's birthright for a bowl of stew (Gen. 25:31–33). We often look at Jacob's early years with judgment for his actions, but the truth is that his behavior was taught to him by his family members. Jacob's family had a history of hustling. When Jacob's father, Isaac, was getting old, it was Jacob's mother, Rebekah, who told him to fool his father and take the blessing from Isaac that belonged to his brother, Esau (Gen. 27). Rebekah helps her son fool his old man into giving him a blessing! When Jacob has to flee from Esau because of Jacob's deceitful behavior, Rebekah sends Jacob to stay with her brother Laban, who later makes an arrangement with Jacob to marry his daughter Rachel for seven years of hard work (Gen. 29:16–30). But after the work is over, when the time comes for Jacob to marry his dream girl, his uncle pulls a fast one and has him marry his other daughter Leah first! Laban says he can have Rachel, but he's got to work for seven more years to get her! When we look at Jacob's behavior, it's not difficult to see where he learned it from when we look at a sneaky mother and an angle-working uncle.

BREAKING CLEAN

Our natural instinct is to repeat patterns our families taught us, consciously or unconsciously. When we understand what being a product of our family truly means, we have to take that information into consideration when we are in relationship with someone else. Essentially, we are carrying our family into our relationship with us, and all of those things, good and bad, will come into play in our marriage. Our parents or people of influence in our family of origin were mentors in our relationship development. We will deal with this issue more completely in chapter 4, but the influence of race and institutional racism on a family can have a significant effect on the family's interactions and approach to different issues.

Couples need to understand their own family's behavioral patterns and not expect their spouses to have the same background and behaviors. Wives who have not had healthy relationships with their fathers because they were emotionally unavailable or absent can expect their husbands to validate their sense of worth and take care of them in some unreasonable ways. Husbands who have enmeshed or extremely close relationships with their mothers may expect their wives to provide and take care of them in the same way their mothers did—that may not be reasonable or feasible for their wives to accomplish. The issues and contracts we've established with our families of origin can carry into our marriage relationships and create serious tensions with a couple's development.

Murray Bowen, a noted family systems therapist, developed the concept of understanding the process of *differentiation*. Simply put, differentiation is the healthy process of managing our thinking versus our feeling. People who are well-differentiated can process their feelings for just what they are, feelings that come from their experiences, their families of origins, their thought patterns, and their lives. Well-differentiated people understand that their feelings are not necessarily everyone's feelings. "Well-differentiated people carefully consider pros and cons of various choices. They are able to make rational decisions because they distinguish between their thoughts and feelings. They do not insist that others live by their beliefs and they are less likely to become either defensive or aggressive with someone who has different beliefs."[2] To be well-differentiated is to understand that everyone doesn't think like you, react like you, respond like you, or work like you. You are less focused on getting people to do what you think they should do because you understand there are more ways to look at handling the challenges of life.

When we are well-differentiated in marriage we will work to see our spouse's perspective. We can feel strongly about something but still respect our spouse's approach and perspective even if we don't agree. Well-differentiated people will try hard not to take the disagreement of a spouse personally. The fact that their partner has a different opinion will not be interpreted as "They don't care about me" or "They don't love me," but the person will recognize that they can see things differently and still have care and concern for each other.

Some of us hold on tight to the legacies from our families of origin and work hard to make sure that those thoughts, behaviors, and patterns stay in place. We might be loyal to our families of origin for several different reasons, and when what we have been taught or raised with has been challenged, we can sometimes become defensive and even confrontational. The comment or critique of our thoughts and the way we do things can be interpreted as an attack or insult to our families. Sometimes, because of our loyalties, we can become undifferentiated in our responses and approaches to our relationships. "People who are not well-differentiated are unable to make the distinction between thinking and feeling. They may be able to perform well in the work world, or when performing thing-oriented tasks, as opposed to people-oriented tasks, but such careful functioning is totally lost when dealing with intimate relationships. They are extremely sensitive and easily hurt. For the sake of the relationship, many make compromises that they would not make if they felt more secure about their identity."[3] When we are not well-differentiated in our relationships, we can take everything personally. We can feel like our spouse is uncaring or inconsiderate because they do not see things the way we see them. We take offense to them not agreeing with us, and in the event we do not want to be hurt or disappointed, we go along with a spouse's perspective or opinion because we do not want to be let down or be made to feel that our idea or perspective isn't good enough or well received.

THE NEW FOUNDATION

The great misconception of many people is believing that they can disassociate from all prior family connections and be able to establish a life with a new individual as a healthy and whole person. However, the reality is that we cannot escape our past experiences and family connections. Unfortunately, some of our wounds and scars from our families or past relationships have caused us to turn inward, and we hide and don't share our feelings with others, even those who are close to us. This can create greater friction in marriages—especially when we are so emotionally shut off that we cannot find ways to connect to our spouses. We can relate with our spouses in practical ways and on a surface level, but we never really open ourselves to the point where we allow ourselves to be vulnerable in their presence.

In Genesis we find, "For this reason a man will leave his father and mother and be united to his wife" (2:24). Some take that to mean all ties should be cut off from our families to build relationship with our spouses. I do not believe the text implies terminating family ties, but it does encourage healthy separation as a way to create a healthy future. When we talk about separating from our family, we need to look at how we interpret the secrets, legacies, and contracts that our families have passed down to us. We need to determine a healthy look at the things we have experienced that are both helpful and detrimental to our wellness. Everything that we've learned from our family isn't negative; in fact, some of the things that help us parent, maintain romance, and support each other in the home are very good lessons. We need to know what has been helpful to us and keep those lessons alive. As far as things that may present themselves as negative, we first need to be honest with ourselves and recognize that there are some things that we need to leave behind. We do not have to honor the legacies of abuse, neglect, abandonment, criticism, or lack of support. How we do that is by understanding that we do not have to take on those traits and behaviors as our own. We can recognize that parents make mistakes, that choices are sometimes made incorrectly, and that their mistakes do not have to become our life patterns. Many of those feelings will not go away overnight, and some will require significant work, but if we want to be healthy and responsible to the relationship we are trying to build, we will be willing to make that commitment. When we are honest and face those secrets and understand that we no longer have to continue to carry those legacies, we can then seriously discuss and begin to examine what new thoughts and patterns we can use to help replace the negative thinking and actions of our past.

When we understand that we can be free from some of the legacies in our past that are negative, we can open ourselves up to be receptive to love and companionship from each other. When we don't see who we are or what we come to the relationship with as deficiencies, and when we don't have to be judgmental about one another's approaches to the issues of life, we can then begin to understand how seeing another perspective can be helpful to the advancement of the relationship as a whole. Understanding ourselves helps us to be better people in our relationships as we grow together. When we are balanced and recognize what we are bringing to the relationship and are willing to be open to other perspectives and views, we can remove some of the conflict that may arise in the beginning years of marriage.

Questions to Discuss Together

1. If you have met each others' families, talk about any behaviors you believe your partner inherited from her or his family.
2. How did your parent(s) deal with conflict? Describe a conflict you can remember and what happened.

3. In what ways are you similar to your family, and what, if anything, would you like to change about ways you deal with conflict or stress?

Action Step

Each of you make a list of negative and positive behaviors you learned from your family of origin that you wish to change or repeat. Spend some time talking about your list together.

NOTES

4

Becoming Conscious

The Legacy of African American Relationships

> When you follow in the path of your father, you learn to walk like him.
> —Ashanti Proverb

> Whoever gets sense loves his own soul; he who keeps understanding will discover good.
> —Proverbs 19:8 (ESV)

African Americans cannot properly examine what we bring to our relationships without examining the story of African American marriages and relationships historically. As we talk about the legacies we carry with us through our personal families, we must realize that our culture plays a factor. The legacy of African American relationships is a tale of tragedy and triumph. The dictates of the system of slavery in which we arrived in this developing country, mixed in with the multigenerational effects of institutional and systemic racism, have created a unique perspective in the way African Americans view relationships. There have been families that would be considered the typical nuclear unit, with both parents in the home and 2.5 children and a white picket fence and a dog named Skipper. But there have also been families in the African American community that have not been typical, families of children that have been raised by single parents, grandparents, other family members, or even non-family members. Whatever type of family unit in the African American community we come from, we should acknowledge that those who have a desire to connect with each other through the marriage relationship come from some variation of the family system, and through that system, a system that still operates out of the backdrop of race, class, and culture in America, there will be challenges.

The challenges that face African American relationships ultimately stem from the multigenerational legacy of racism and slavery. The history of slavery has in many cases been well-documented but not particularly well understood by the masses, both African American and white, in terms of the long-lasting and the still-lingering effects on people of African descent. The emotional and psychological wounds still linger in the psyches of African Americans today. These issues of dealing with self-identity, issues of inferiority, negative imaging, and empowerment have effects on African Americans in all aspects of life. How relationships and marriages in African American communities are affected is no exception. The legacy of marriage and family in the African American community still struggles to identify itself because of the history that racism has produced. Even now, as many have progressed professionally and, as a result, economically, the struggle to identify for African Americans what it means to be in a healthy relationship can vary greatly. Many African American men and women find it difficult to connect with each other when it comes to having a lasting and long-term commitment. Issues of economics, shared goals and ideas, professional status, education, prior children, and so on can be deal breakers for the person looking for a partner in marriage. As a result, many individuals are selecting to live together or have short-term "arrangements" with individuals with no sense of committing to anything long term. More women are deciding that if they cannot find someone to marry but want to have children, they will be single mothers, and they may or may not have plans to include the father of the child in the parenting experience. The understanding of what being in a committed relationship means has become incredibly fluid, and the parameters for marriage can vary from person to person.

At the risk of taking this book in a whole other direction, my role at this point is not to take a stance on all of these issues but to help us take an honest look at what we have experienced historically regarding marriage, as well as identify the origin of these perspectives.

Sidney and JoAnn have been to see me before. Their "on-again-off-again" romance was beginning to come to some kind of a head. They planned to marry in a few months, but they needed a few more sessions before they took their final step.

> **Pastor:** Sid, you look disturbed, my brother, what's on your mind?
>
> **Sidney:** I was let go at my job, and with this wedding coming, I know we're going to need money.
>
> **Pastor:** Do you have any leads on any jobs?
>
> **Sidney:** No, you know how construction is. I'm trying to work some things out, but I just have to wait and see.
>
> **Pastor:** JoAnn, what do you think about all of this? This has got to be frustrating for you as well.
>
> **JoAnn:** It is, but you know, we just have to wait until something comes up. I keep telling him he needs to go back to school, so he can have something to fall back on.
>
> **Sidney:** I told you school has never been my thing. I make good money. I've never been without. I make a good living. School is your thing.
>
> **JoAnn:** It's not like I'm making him, I just keep making the suggestion. I know he's making good money and all, but I'm just not comfortable with the working here and working there work schedules. I just want to make sure that I have some help in this thing. I don't want to be one of those sisters who ends up taking care of everything, including her husband, you know?

Sidney: Take care of me? When have you ever taken care of me? My job may be on again off again, like you say, but I have never been without, and neither have you! You don't seem to mind when the money is coming in. How are you going to sit here and think you are going to take care of me?

JoAnne and Sidney are having the same conversation many African American men and women have with their friends on Friday nights at happy hour. JoAnn, who is college educated, wants to have a husband who has an education as well. To her, education represents stability. JoAnn and Sidney struggle with the images and stereotypes of African American relationships. JoAnn doesn't want to "take care" of a man, which she believes is a possibility when it comes to African American men, and Sidney doesn't want to be labeled as a shiftless, lazy, unproductive man. Sidney also feels understandably unhappy in some ways about his being out of work. In his eyes, he should always be working and productive, and his being laid off not only effects how he feels about himself but also potentially affects what happens in his relationship. Sidney and JoAnn's situation is temporary, and their relationship can work through this rough period. However, they need to understand that because of the dynamics of their relationship structure, unless other changes are made, this is something they will have to constantly work on.

AFRICAN RELATIONSHIPS THROUGH HISTORY

Many images of the continent of Africa have shown an undeveloped continent of unlimited resources but display a very limited, and often negative, understanding of its people. Thoughts about "the dark continent" give impressions of savage people with no social structure or morals of any significance or value. The missionaries who came along with the slave traders may have claimed to perceive an uncivilized, barbaric, and godless people, but they could not have been further from the truth. African traditions and customs existed long before the slave traders had ever made it to the African shores. There were and continue to be many empires and communities that function and operate under a clear sense of order, and included in all the other societal structures was the structure of family.

Marriage in most African villages was, and is, a communal event. The couples themselves were not just connecting, but it was viewed as an additional joining of the community. The village operated as a unit, and the married couple was a part of that unit. "Since the individual exists only because the corporate group exists, it is vital that in this most important contract of life, other members of that corporate community must get involved in the marriage of the individual."[1] The covenant of marriage was understood to be a relevant step in the African community, because it promoted unity, stability, and growth.

The focus of the Trans-Atlantic slave trade was to have free labor for producing the goods in the agricultural society that was the developing Americas and the West Indies. To that end, the family structure of Africans in America was a nonissue as far as the Europeans were concerned, but the use of Black bodies as chattel was not. It was imperative that African slaves produce children as a labor resource, but marriage among Africans was not legally recognized.

The relationships of African men and women started to become strained. Women, whether they were field hands or working in the house, could be subjected to all types of physical abuse and brutality. Because African women were seen as property, slaveholders could do whatever they chose with the enslaved, which included sexual violence. As a man, the psychological trauma of not being able to do anything while your wife is being defiled and abused by your slave owner was, needless to say, devastating. Along with their psychological torture of feeling powerless to do anything to protect their women, they had little power in regard to providing for the women as well. According to Patricia Dixon, in the book *African American Relationships, Marriages and Families*, "the slaveholder provided the cabin, clothing, and food, and it was typically through the woman. This made it not only impossible for African American men to be providers for their families, but essentially made them invisible or nonbeings in their households."[2]

The most devastating blow to the African marriage relationship may have been the separation of families. The possibility of being sold away from your family was a constant fear that continued to linger daily. The selling of family members could be done for profit or for punishment. The decision belonged entirely to the slaveholder, the owner, with no input whatsoever from the Africans themselves. But no matter how traumatic the erratic and violent slaveholder's treatment was, the family still served as the place of hope for the African. Mixing African and American cultures, many of the communal rituals and practices created bonds of connectedness despite the atmosphere in which the community was forced to exist. The marriage relationship, even though it wasn't acknowledged legally by the slaveholder, served as a place of refuge and safety for enslaved Africans.

THE STRUGGLE CONTINUES

With the end of slavery in 1865, freed Africans found themselves searching for not only a way to survive but also for individual and collective identities. As a result, we find ourselves as African Americans still wrestling, in many ways, with the pains and scars of the slavery issue. Like all traumatic experiences, if not effectively dealt with, the trauma can manifest itself in many different ways and affect several generations. As with all unresolved issues, the discussion of marriage in the African American community continues to find itself at the center of what it means to be healthy.

What seems to be our struggle is understanding the perception of who we are, and ultimately who are we supposed to be within our marriages and relationships. If we have not come to a place where we are comfortable with ourselves, then how can we believe that we can be comfortable with someone in a marriage partnership? How do we see each other as potential marriage partners? What qualities do we see as beneficial in the world of African American relationships?

We tell our children when they begin to date what to share, how much to let on, to protect their feelings and not to give too much of themselves away because you don't know how the relationship is going to end up. We train ourselves to become guarded. We condition ourselves to have an easy out. We can like someone, but to keep from getting ourselves hurt, we will live in the "friend zone." We don't want to tell the people we care about we have feelings for them until they share first because we don't want to make the first move. We are conditioned to live and behave a certain way when it comes to relationships, but what we really have done is blocked ourselves from receiving what we really want, and that is authentic connection. We find ourselves caught up in the games of relationships, and these practices can carry on even in our marriages because of the perceptions that we have both learned and been taught about women and men.

VIEWS AND OPINIONS OF MEN AND WOMEN

When it comes to African American men, there are many perceptions that are shared in the minds of women and the American culture. These perceptions were initially perpetuated by the society in which we live. What has happened is these images have now become assumptions, and we run the risk of believing that all men or at least most of them operate in these descriptions.

African American men have been viewed as angry, inherently violent, sexually obsessed, lazy if not properly motivated, emotionally empty but physically virile individuals who know how to make children but somehow or another are incapable of taking care of them without significant shaming or help.

Images of African American men can often be thought of as threatening or menacing with the inference being that they are more predator than person. Stereotypes of African American men include the misrepresentation that their sexual prowess is so intense that they cannot simply survive with just one partner. This fiction makes men useful in the bedroom but unfortunately, for many, that is as far as any usefulness goes. It is also perceived that men have no interest in serious intimacy or any form of emotional connection. It is believed that African American men expect to be taken care of by women, and when things get emotionally heavy, the men disappear.

The image perpetuated by society is tragically reinforced with the help of images from TV, film, and through musical genres, such as hip-hop culture, known for its misogynistic overtones and images of male domination and the exploitation and disrespect of women. These images contribute to the feelings African American men experience as they attempt to connect with others in society and the women with whom they hope to be in relationship. The devaluation of African American men did not stop with the emancipation of slavery, but it has continued to perpetuate itself in current culture. These images help to perpetuate negative stereotypes and can be detrimental not only in the societal sense, but they can affect relationships as well.

African American women are not exempt from the negative images and stereotypes of society. Often depicted as angry, argumentative, uptight, too independent, money-hungry, and sexually promiscuous, African American women also fight against negative sexual narratives. These storylines stem from the history and relationship of the African woman and the slave-owner. The inference is that African American women have very little sexual discretion and are available to have sex with any and every man. The images of surface, shallow women looking for handouts or someone to take care of them, and their children, is not only an inaccurate depiction, it degrades those who are genuinely working and living healthy lives and relationships.

WHAT IS REAL?

What can make marriage relationships difficult for African American couples is that they have to contend with the negative imaging of African American men and women as portrayed in society, along with the perceptions that have been taught and infused in their psyches from the lessons their families have shared with them. This all on top of the experiences that individuals have had through past relationships. If a young boy has been taught by the male members of his family that he should watch his money around women because all women try to get a man's money, and this idea is further reinforced by images of women in music videos flocking around men fanning themselves with one hundred dollar bills, he will enter into his relationships with women cautious about women's attitude toward money. If, or when, she brings up finances or is focused on achieving certain things, he will immediately refer to what he's been taught and exposed to and either remain more guarded or exit the relationship altogether.

If a woman has been told all her life that all African American men are dogs and constantly cheat on you and if every movie she watches portrays a black man having an affair, it is likely that she will carry that into her relationships with her. As a result, every time her man goes out to the grocery store or goes to work or hangs out with his friends, somewhere in the back of her mind, she wonders where he really is. If he is late coming home without a phone call, a negative interpretation can take place and a situation that could be a simple matter can escalate quickly into something stressful and unnecessary. Now, obviously, this is not true for all scenarios and relationships, but the point is that if there is a pattern of negative thinking about relationships and the opposite sex due to cultural influence, family life lessons, past relationships, or a combination of any of the three, it can create frustrating and difficult times for any couple.

The influence of family and society is powerful on relationships. When people share or give advice about the opposite sex, they are often speaking from personal experiences, so it is important to discern between wounded advice and objective insight. It is difficult to avoid people's input in relationships, especially the input of family and those close to us, but it is necessary to see people as individuals and not as stereotypes. Wrestling with the images and stereotypes of family and society puts limits on our ability to be open and understanding in a new relationship. Buying into those stereotypes limits the possibility of knowing who a person can truly be by already assuming who they are.

Questions to Discuss Together

1. How has the media (i.e., movies, TV, music) affected your image of African American men and women? How do you think this affects your expectation of your partner?
2. The author makes the point that, due to the history of African Americans in this country, many men and women are afraid to commit to a relationship. Has this been your experience? Explain.
3. Describe the qualities of a "good" spouse.

Action Step

Find a movie you can see, or a book you can read, together that deals with some of the history and content of this chapter. After reading the book or viewing the movie, discuss how the experience of African Americans in this country might affect you as a couple.

NOTES

5

Becoming Mature

Turning Mourning into Morning

There is nothing like the excitement of wedding planning. So
many things need to be done. Calls to caterers, bakers, and
banquet halls must be made. Decisions about ceremony par-
ticipants, and what they will wear, must be considered. The
planning can be exciting and exhausting at the same time.
When it comes to the wedding, couples often have big plans
and even bigger dreams, but that is not always the case with
the marriage. The wedding day is indeed special, but much
more attention should be paid to the life that you are about
to begin together. It is essential to recognize that a wedding is
not a marriage. The work of the marriage ceremony is not the
work of the marriage.

Obviously, a new marriage takes an adjustment period, and
some things can be worked out and processed through good
communication and flexibility, just two of the marriage qualities we will look at in the second half of this book. There are
some adjustments that will need to take place not just with the
way you communicate with one another, but also the ways in
which you view marriage. Many new couples find themselves
aggravated, upset, frustrated, and even wanting to throw in the

towel early because what they thought marriage was and what they have come to discover marriage is are two entirely different things. The adjustment period of marriage is not just about learning about your spouse, it is also about unlearning the preconceived notions about what we believed marriage would be. When we realize life will not be like we envisioned it in our heads for so many years before the marriage, we find ourselves in a place of mourning.

Mourning is the period in any process when we feel or express feelings of sorrow or grief. We have this period mostly due to a feeling of loss that forces change. We often use the term mourning for the death of an individual that we are close to or familiar with but, in reality, we mourn many different things when change occurs in our lives. When we come into marriages with ideas of who our spouse is and what our relationship will look like and those ideas quickly have to change, we mourn the fact that what were once lifelong dreams are never coming to pass.

Maya and Rasheed had been married a few months when they asked to come and see me. I had performed the wedding and in the back of my mind wondered what they wanted to talk about. When they came in, they both seemed deep in thought, and as they went to sit down, Rasheed sat in a chair next to the sofa in my office, Maya sat on the sofa. Because I knew them a little bit, I immediately addressed the seating arrangement: "Hey Rasheed, you want to sit next to your bride?" He responded respectfully but somewhat sarcastically, "I don't know, I'm not sure she wants me to." I looked at Maya and tested the waters. "Maya, why does Rasheed think you don't want him to sit next to you?" She looked at me and her eyes started to well up with tears. I couldn't tell if she was embarrassed to be in my office or hurt by Rasheed's move to sit away from her. She responded in a shaky voice: "Because that's how he's been acting lately." I asked her, "How do you feel he's been acting?" "*Ugly!*" She blurted out, "He is so mean! I've never met anyone so mean in my life, he just says what he wants to say, and he acts like it doesn't hurt or like he doesn't

care." I looked at Rasheed, and his face was blank, like he had
heard this a hundred times before. He didn't look like he was
moved by her mixture of tears and anger. "Rasheed, what do
you think about what Maya said? She seems kind of hurt right
now." Rasheed looked at Maya when he spoke: "I think she's
over exaggerating; it's really not that serious." "It's serious
enough to her that she is in tears, wouldn't you think that was
serious enough?" He responded in frustration. "I mean yeah, I
don't want to see her unhappy. I don't like to see her cry, but
she is always crying! I mean *always*! It doesn't matter what it is,
whatever we talk about, if I don't agree, I'm being mean—how
do you live with that?" I noticed Maya wiping her face. "Maya,
why does talking to your husband upset you?" "Because he
doesn't know how to talk to people. I am not one of his sol-
diers. I'm not one of the people under his command; you don't
bark orders at me, I am not in the military. I am his wife, and
he should know the difference." I began to try to put some type
of framing around the issue: "It sounds like we're talking about
figuring out how we talk to each other and understanding what
is fair to say and what is not fair to say to one another. Is that
something we can take time to discuss?" There was silence in
the room, and Maya's folded arms stayed firmly at her sides as
she looked at me. Finally, Rasheed spoke up. "I don't know,
Pastor, I just don't understand what's going on. I talk the way
I've always talked. I have been this way all my life. I have to get
things done. I have to make tough decisions. I'm a keep-it-real
kind of dude. I don't know why, all of a sudden, the way I talk
is a problem. I mean I knew she was sensitive, but it was never
like this before now."

After six months of marriage, Rasheed and Maya are strug-
gling with their relationship realities. Maya really didn't know
that Rasheed could be so aggressive, and Rasheed didn't know
that Maya's sensitivity was so great. No doubt they had seen
these attributes in each other before this moment, but they did
not, for whatever reason, want to see them as a potential issue.
To both Rasheed and Maya, this is who they have always been,
and the other person accepted who they were by marrying

them, and to be upset or to ask them to change the way they are is upsetting because it feels like the other person is changing the arrangement.

What couples need to know is that this behavior pattern really isn't uncommon. Some couples handle it better than others, but all relationships in their early stages face the same thing. We come to the reality that the person we were marrying is not the person we thought they were; in fact, there are many more layers to them than we realized. "Each of us constructs an idealized image of the person we marry. The image is planted by our partner's eager efforts to put his best foot forward, but it takes root in the rich soil of our romantic fantasies. We want to see our partner at his best. We imagine, for example, that he would never become irritable or put on excess weight. We seek out and attend to what we find admirable and blank out every blemish. We see him as more noble, more attractive, more intelligent, more gifted than he really is. But not for long."[1] We worked hard to create the idea and the image in our head of who we were with, we polished it and shined it up for everyone to see, but somewhere along the way reality set in, and now they somehow don't seem as shiny as they used to be. We can feel all types of feelings when we come to the realization that our partner is not who we thought they were. We can feel somehow the person wasn't honest with us, that we've found ourselves trapped in a relationship that we had no plans to be in with a person we never knew existed, and we can have all kinds of negative responses in the process.

Couples who begin to feel that they are not with the person they initially thought can begin to create distance. They can do that through creating conflict with their spouse, picking fights so that they don't have to deal with their partner intimately. People can put their energies into other things and find other interests. Some start to hang out with their friends more and their spouses less. All of these reactions and others are escapes that prevent people from dealing with the real issues. Being married is a part of understanding the commitment to maturity and dealing with things so that as a couple you can continue to

move forward. Many of the escape mechanisms will only tem-
porarily relieve the stress of the relationship and could possibly
bring even more stress to the marriage. "You can't have a great
marriage if one or both of you is not showing up as a grown-
up. You can have a wedding. You can even be married for fifty
years. But it won't be a great marriage."[2] People have to be
willing to engage in dealing with the challenges and changes
of marriage, because there will continue to be both throughout
the journey of your relationship.

WHAT ARE WE REALLY SEEING?

When we come to the reality of a relationship and discover that
our marriage is not going to be what we imagined and dreamed
it would be, we mourn the death of our dream. However, the
dream that we had, for all intents and purposes, was an unrealistic dream to begin with. The reason why the dream we had
about our marriage should be a particular way is based on two
very real factors.

The first factor is that we came up with an idea of what
marriage was going to be in our own heads with our own ideas,
never considering that there was going to be someone else in
the picture who was going to have her own set of ideas and
dreams about what marriage was going to be like. The second factor that we don't consider in our pursuit for our dream
relationship is that in our dream marriage, our dream spouse
is doing everything we imagined he would do and being everything we imagined he would be. We often imagine how our
partner will treat us, but we never consider our own responsibilities, we never have to do anything or contribute anything
in our dreams. Our dreams are about the wonderful people we
create in our heads, including us. We don't consider our dream
spouses' faults and shortcomings, and we sure don't consider
our own. We know about our issues and hang-ups, but we
never consider that they would get on our spouse's nerves.
We know our personality "hitches" and idiosyncrasies, but we

never for a second think that our "stuff" would be annoying, disturbing, or even nerve-racking to our spouses. In our fantasy idea of marriage, we want to put rules and parameters on the people we choose for mates and expect them to stay within our lines, but we want our spouses to love us unconditionally and not acknowledge any of the personality or behavioral struggles we have. That's why the early stages of marriage can be so challenging, because our spouses force us to see the things we don't like about ourselves. "The merged life of marriage brings you into the closest, most inescapable contract with another person possible. And that means not only that you see each other close up, but that you are forced to deal with the flaws and sins of one another."[3] The relationship of marriage forces us to come to the realization that not only is our partner not perfect, but based on their frustration, obviously neither are we.

As one who performs marriages, I am in total agreement with what Dr. Robin Smith says: "The first marriage vow should be: *I promise to show up as a grown-up*. Not as a little girl fulfilling a fantasy, not as a nervous boy doing what he's supposed to do. Not as Prince Charming or Lady Bountiful. Not as the fulfillment of your mother's expectations. Not as the envy of all your friends."[4] Understanding what it means to have a great marriage is to recognize that you have to be an adult. Like children, adults have dreams, but unlike children, adults understand that for dreams to become reality they require real work, diligence, and sometimes compromise. The dream you should be working on is to have a healthy and successful marriage, not the idea of the marriage you have in your head. The grown-up marriage realizes that it is not only about you, but it is about understanding that someone else has a part in this process.

Being a grown-up means that you also understand the challenges that you bring to the relationship. You have some things that you yourself need to work on. What can be the most difficult for couples is for people to think that their issues can go untreated and their spouse has to make all the adjustments. Most couples, when they come in to see me with their frustrations, point to each other and want me to "fix" him or her, because obviously they are the one that has the problem. I am quick to point out that as they point to the other person to call out their faults and flaws, that there are three other fingers pointing back at them on the same self-righteous hand. It is important to know what struggles you as an individual have and know what things challenge you. Because here's the news flash: the only person you can work on in a relationship is you. The only person you can change in a relationship is you, and the only person you can do anything about in terms of behavior in a relationship is you. So often we think that if we can just get our spouses to change, everything will be all right, when the real issue is not necessarily what your spouse is doing, but your behavior, attitude, and response to what your spouse is doing, that will ultimately make the difference.

THE PROCESS OF "MOURNING"

When we come to the realization that certain things won't be as we initially thought in our marriage relationship, we tend to get down and upset about it. We are in what I call a mourning period, a time when we understand that our vision or idea of marriage will not become a reality. It is a sad time for individuals, no doubt, but if handled correctly, one that can be survived. Mourning is a part of any growth process. Whenever we find ourselves in the middle of change and growth, there will be things we will have to let go. There will be things that we will have to lose. There will be adjustments that need to be made and ideas that won't make it with us. All of that is how we have a grown-up look at marriage, realizing that what we had won't be the same way anymore, even if what we had was only in our imaginations.

In the Bible, Samuel is having a problem adjusting to the fact that Saul will no longer be king. This is no small thing for Samuel because Saul was the man that he had anointed with oil (1 Sam. 10:1). Samuel had great faith in Saul. In fact, Samuel had talked with God, and even though Samuel was reluctant, God told him to give the people a king (1 Sam. 8:21). Samuel thought that the selection of Saul was God-sent, and it was, but something happened in the process. Due to other circumstances, Saul didn't turn out to be the person Samuel thought he would be, and when Saul violated the instructions of the Lord, God was not pleased with him. As a result, God told Samuel that Saul would not stay the king for much longer. The Bible says that Samuel mourned for Saul. Samuel was grieving that Saul was not going to be king and that God's hand was no longer on him as king. When God speaks to Samuel, he asks him, "How long will you mourn for Saul, since I have rejected him as king over Israel? Fill your horn with oil and be on your way; I am sending you to Jesse of Bethlehem. I have chosen one of his sons to be king" (1 Sam. 16:1).

Samuel had an idea of what Saul's reign as king would be like, and he had no idea that his dream would go sour. Samuel had invested time and prayer in Saul's future, and things looked good at first. Samuel must have been excited that he had made the right choice. Samuel must have been proud when he anointed Saul and thought that he had done well for the people of God. What Samuel wasn't expecting was that Saul would turn out to be different than when he started out. Samuel thought Saul would always stay on the same path, but his idea didn't work out. Because things had to change, Samuel was in mourning. Saul wasn't dead, at least not yet anyway, but Samuel still mourned. God tells Samuel, "Fill your horn with oil and be on your way." God is telling Samuel that although it won't work out like you thought it would, I still have a plan for the people. Even though the person has changed, the people still have a future. God lets Samuel know you can't spend too much time grieving over what wasn't or what isn't going to be, but you can take what God has given you and work with things as they are.

All of us can get disappointed that what we hoped for isn't going to happen, and we can even find ourselves grieving about those things. We can feel a sense of sorrow and grief over the ideas and dreams of our minds. What helps us make it through our mourning process is recognizing that God has not taken away the promise. The promise of a good and healthy marriage is still with us. Our challenge in marriage is to not so much get caught up in what we did not get, or our idea of marriage not working out, but our challenge is to discover the new world that God is opening up to us to see what kind of marriage we can create in the right now. The time of dreaming of what marriage will be is over. The reality of what we help our marriage become is now on us, and we have the opportunity to grow and create a new and exciting relationship. However, before this happens, we must go through the process of grieving the realities of our relationship and come to grips with understanding that it will not be what we imagined it will be.

Elisabeth Kubler-Ross examined the process of grief and proposed that we handle grief in five stages. We process grief in the stages of *denial, anger, bargaining, depression,* and finally *acceptance.* These particular stages are not just dealing with death itself, but all types of experiences when loss is experienced. In the process of understanding our new marriages, we experience these stages sometimes without even realizing it. "We all have coping mechanisms that cover up pain, help us deal with fear, cope with relational inabilities, and help us hold it all together. Trials and suffering push those mechanisms past the breaking point so we find out where we need to grow."[5] These stages of grief take us through our process of mourning. The goal is not to escape the sadness but to live fully and deal with the loss. Only then can we come to accept change.

A NEW "MORNING"

There are all kinds of disappointments in life. We have all experienced things not working out like we planned them, things not happening as we expected, but in those moments, we've managed to look at the bright side, find another option, or change our course entirely. We've managed to find our way back to some kind of path. The challenges of new marriages are similar. We will find ourselves in some situations that we weren't expecting; there will be some changes that we will have to make that we weren't looking for; and there will be some dreams that will be shattered by the reality of our spouse's unique personality. However, these disappointments don't have to be permanent. These realizations can be the stepping stones on which the foundation of a solid, healthy marriage can be built on. We have to go through the process of knowing who we really are, and that can sometimes be difficult, but it is a healing process as well. The fact is, some things need to end for new healthy things to begin. But some pain is beneficial for us. Some experiences, although difficult, bless us through the process. We can experience the same kind of benefit through difficulties, even in our relationships.

> Because grief is God's way of getting finished with the bad stuff of life. It is the process by which we "get over it" by which we "let it go." And because of that, because it is the process by which things can be "over with" it becomes the process by which we can be available for new, good things. The soul is freed from painful experience and released for new, good experience.[6]

When we understand with a level of maturity that the way we see our marriage is just the way we see it, and we can open ourselves up to the realization that our spouse also has not only a view of this relationship but an investment in it as well, we can also open ourselves up and give ourselves permission to release what we are holding onto in terms of ideas and past dreams and begin to build the life we are intended to build with our spouse. The commitment we made at the wedding was not to walk into a "ready-made" life together, but it was that we would build a life together. To truly be a partner means that you should be willing to let some of what you expected go and create something new in the process. Here is the hard part, and that is we must make the investment and do the work of becoming married. We have to trust God in the process and believe that God's plan for our marriage is better than the idea to which we've been holding on. We thought our way would be simple, our way toward marriage would be beneficial to us and individuals, our way would be comfortable, with no bumps and bruises and no hairpin turns in the road. God's way means we should get uncomfortable; God's way means we should see ourselves for who we really are and then do the work on ourselves. God's way means we will have to apologize, ask for forgiveness, recognize when we've messed up, ask for help, and most difficult of all, be vulnerable. God's way exposes more of us, but the good news is that's exactly what we have to do in order to have great marriages. Our mourning can turn into a new morning if we allow ourselves to open up, let go, and become willing to build a new dream, this time one that includes the partner we've made our commitment to.

Questions to Discuss Together

1. What, if anything, have you already mourned in your relationship? That is, what have you had to accept that you did not think you would have to?
2. What do you think about the statement that the first marriage vow should be to show up as a grown-up? What does that mean for you?
3. What are things you need to work on in your marriage?

Action Step

Discuss how communication and flexibility can help you down the road to deal with unmet expectations as a couple.

NOTES

PART TWO

Becoming Qualities: Characteristics that Help Couples Become Married

6

Becoming Self-Aware

Know Thyself

He who loves the vase loves also what's inside.
—African Proverb

The wisdom of the prudent is to discern his way, but the folly of fools is deceiving.
—Proverbs 14:8 (ESV)

We have examined some of the thoughts and theories that affect how two people become a couple and some of the components that come into play in the development of relationships. All of these things factor into how you handle conflict, time, and intimacy in marriage. You may have picked up this book expecting a chapter on money, a chapter on dealing with in-laws, maybe one on family planning. Sorry. While these are issues every couple will face, the purpose of this book is to help identify the underlying qualities that will help couples succeed in marriage.

One of the many issues individuals in relationships deal with is the desire to be a priority in someone else's life. When a person feels like they matter to their spouse, they are more likely to work through situations and conflicts. The qualities discussed in this chapter are traits that can help people in relationships work toward feeling like a priority to each other. If as a couple you work on these components of your marriage, you will be better able to face the issues that will most certainly surface in your marriage.

UNDERSTANDING WHO YOU ARE

Who are you, truly? Beyond your name, and other markers that identify you, who are you? To answer this seemingly simple question, you have to be self-aware. But what does that mean? To be self-aware, you must possess knowledge about your character, your desires, your motives, feelings, and perspectives about life. When you are self-aware you are able, to some degree, to understand why you do the things you do. In his book *Know Thyself*, Dr. Na'im Akbar says, "The process of looking inside of ourselves and remembering the experiences we have had and how those experiences have helped to make us the people that we are is an important part of the self-knowledge process."[1] You should know, this is not an easy thing to do. If you truly seek self-awareness, you have to examine key moments of your life, and some of those memories may not be pleasant to remember. But why should you take this potentially uncomfortable journey? One reason, which is directly related to the goals of this book, is because this process will help you identify your personality traits. As you understand how and why you react to things the way you do, that will help you understand your responses to your spouse and your reactions to issues within your marriage. Think about it like this: You enter a relationship as an individual. If you know who you are as an individual, you will be better able to work with your mate as you become a couple. Some people get married so they can forget who they are, with the hope that their partner will somehow wipe away all of the issues and pain of past relationships. The truth is, however, if the issues of your past are not properly addressed, you will never be healed and ultimately never be whole.

Lynn and Derrick have been married for three years. They had what they initially thought was a communication issue. It became clear after just a few minutes in this conversation that communication was not the real issue.

Pastor: Tell me what's going on.

Lynn: Pastor, I try to talk to Derrick and share things with him, but he always has something critical to say in response. At first I tried to ignore it and act like it didn't bother me, but it's getting increasingly worse.

Pastor: Derrick, what is it you feel about what Lynn is saying? Is there any truth to her claims of you being a little too critical?

Derrick: I don't think she's right at all. I don't understand why she gets angry. Am I not supposed to see the holes in her argument? Am I just supposed to let her talk about things incorrectly? I just notice things and I point them out; it's not a big deal.

Pastor: Do you see how it could be a big deal to Lynn? She thinks it comes off kind of critical.

Lynn: It *is* critical! I can't do anything right. I don't clean the kitchen right. I don't buy the right food when I go shopping. I don't even get our daughter dressed in the right order when I dress her—I mean shirt first then pants and shoes, I mean come on, I have to hear about everything!

Derrick: (Laughs) Well, I mean OK, that might be a little OCD. But it's not personal, I mean, I do that because I care about her. I want her to do the best and be the best, and I just want to help her get things right. I don't know why she has to get upset. If she doesn't want my help, then fine, I won't help her.

Pastor: Did you ever think that Lynn has a way of doing things that works for her? Perhaps she's upset because your commenting on what she does so critically causes her to feel that you don't appreciate the effort she's making.

Lynn: *Exactly!* What makes you think that you have all the answers? When you attack me like that,

> I don't feel like you think I can do anything. And I know I work too hard and I am too tired to hear that you don't like the way I do things, because you can do it all by yourself if you don't like how I do things!

The issue that Lynn and Derrick face is more complicated than ineffective communication. Derrick intends for his commentary to help his wife, not to criticize her. Lynn, however, hears Derrick's words as judgment on her abilities as a wife. The answers to why Derrick and Lynn respond to each other the way they do are in their pasts. For the sake of space and time, let us use Derrick as our example in this case.

Derrick's father had a habit of making sure he got things "right," and no mistakes were made. As far as Derrick's father was concerned, the only way to do things "right" was his way. This means Derrick was on the receiving end of a constant barrage of criticism, and because Derrick understood the corrections as "helpful," he believed his father spoke to him in the spirit of love and concern. Unfortunately for Derrick, Lynn did not interpret his actions in the same way. Lynn understood Derrick's criticism as a sign of unhappiness. Through the process of becoming self-aware, Derrick had to learn to recognize the potentially negative nature of his comments.

In a marriage, one of the most important things you can do is understand who you are and what you bring to the relationship. Admitting the truth about yourself and about who you are allows you to truly connect with your spouse. Hiding things about yourself can be damaging to the relationship because by doing so, you are unable to share your true self with your beloved. If you are not willing to open up to your partner about your hopes and fears, they cannot know the real you. Becoming a couple means that you trust your partner with your history and your hurt, and you trust that your spouse will love and care for you, regardless of your past.

TROUBLES BECOMING SELF-AWARE

Becoming self-aware may seem like a simple process, but the task itself can be easier said than done. In marriage, it is easy to get defensive about taking time to understand ourselves better. Marriage can give you an easy scapegoat because you often focus on issues that affect your spouse, but you don't take the same time to examine yourself. But remember, in marriage, it is about becoming a couple, not "fixing" you or your spouse. Think about this process as unlocking a new part of your life. Marriage is not the death of who you are, but it is an addition to the life you are looking to live.

The outside influences of the people you love and respect can be heavy and can follow you into your marriage, whether you want them to or not. This means, if you're not careful, your response to marital situations could be sparked by these influences. Many of your reactions in your relationship will be a result of your beliefs and convictions, and if you don't have a good sense of who you are, you may not even realize what is happening. Some might experience something called *parataxic distortion*, which occurs when you treat your partner as if they were your parent or someone else from your past who has left a lasting impression on you. An example of parataxic distortion: your spouse teases you about something they think is funny, but it makes you angry because someone teased you when you were growing up. We tend to experience triggers in situations when we are stressed out or when our anxiety is high. But when we are self-aware, you can be aware of emotional triggers and you can better manage your reactions and responses.

WHERE TO BEGIN

The purpose of being self-aware in our marriage is to understand ourselves. We cannot be effective in our relationships if we do not have a good understanding of who we are. You've heard it said you can't love others if you first do not love yourself. All of us, in one form or another, have a story of history and hurts. We have a memory of the good and bad things we have gone through, and those events continue on with us. It is important to have a grasp on what has happened so that we might effectively manage our history and not let it control the life of the relationship.

Our self-awareness begins with first a sense of understanding our potential. Our histories and hurts can have us feeling like all that is possible for us is the experiences that we've been through. When we understand the potential of what God can still do with us, we can recognize that there is more in store for us than just the experiences we've had. We need to look at our experiences as lessons to add to our lives, not the definition of what our lives will be. There is an old saying: "I may be guilty of what they said I did, but I am not who they say I am." That statement takes responsibility for where we've been, but it also doesn't limit us to where we can go. We are more than the past experiences of our lives—we have so much more potential. The fact that we are in a marriage relationship stresses that fact. The fact that we are in this relationship means that we believe in possibilities. When we have a spouse who is committed to growing with us each and every day, then we have the possibility and potential to become something more. The gift of marriage lets us know that we aren't limited to the past, but we can still build a bright future.

Being self-aware will help us to see the divine opportunity in others as well. When we see the possibility in ourselves, we have to be able to see it in our spouses as well. If we understand that our past doesn't limit us, then we should be open to the possibility that whatever our spouse has experienced will not limit them either. In marriage, we can begin to see the hand of God's grace in all of us. We can recognize that our partners are not limited by their experiences as well, and we should not hold them hostage to their histories and hurts. We have been touched by the grace of God, and that has opened us up to the freeing possibility of the future and what we can become. Then we need to understand that as a couple, our future can only become when we extend the same possibility of God's grace to our spouses as well.

We cannot limit them in their life potential. Self-awareness helps us see that God's grace is applicable to everyone.

HELPING TO IMPROVE SELF-AWARENESS

Although self-awareness is essential to marital relationships, it is one of those things that must be done by the individual. It is difficult for your spouse to help you become more self-aware, particularly if you don't recognize your need to do so. The work of self-awareness has to be done by the individual because it is the individual who must do the hard work of honest examination of themselves. People who are not self-aware will blame others for what is happening to them and look at everyone else as the problem. Usually this is done because of the fear we have about looking at the past experiences in our lives that are either too painful or too devastating to examine. It is my recommendation that when you find yourself in this reflective period, you find someone to help you work through those difficult memories and help you process your way through them. Many times we can take on the guilt, shame, hurt, or anger of what has happened to us and internalize it and have it reveal itself in many different ways and times. Self-awareness is about coming to terms with what has gone on in your life and understanding your personality, including your strengths as well as your weaknesses. Self-awareness helps us to understand where we are coming from and what our motivations are. Discovering these things can be intimidating, and for some even scary, but becoming more self-aware will help you understand how you approach your marriage and how you deal with situations that arise in your relationship. Some ways you can help yourself become more self-aware are:

Write down your values and the things that really matter to you. These should be things that are important to your individuality. Then take time to figure out where those values came from. Figure out if they came from your family or some other person of influence or perhaps even a situation that happened to you. Use those as your basis for your work.

Ask yourself if you make others around you operate or live by these values. Ask yourself honestly if you are too critical of others who don't follow your rules or if you are judgmental of others who have different approaches than you do.

Make an inventory of the relationships you have had. Friends or intimate relationships count. Have people told you that you have a tendency to be critical or ridgid in some areas? How did you feel when they shared that with you? Were you defensive? Were you angry? Did you see them as being out of touch or misunderstanding you? Did you fall out of relationship with people and you never knew why?

Discover your emotional triggers. What things set you off? This one you might want to ask a close friend or a spouse to help you with. What things do you consider "pet peeves," and how do you react when those things happen?

Work on checking your emotions. Understand what you feel is what you are feeling based on your thoughts and experiences. Come to understand that no one is making you feel anything. Your feelings are based on your interpretation. Do you fly off the handle or get critical with others, or are you able to talk through your thoughts and feelings to get your point across? Can you live with the idea that things may not go your way? Can you operate understanding that other people have their own opinions and approaches to life?

Apologize when necessary. An apology is a wonderful way to acknowledge our limitations. Apologies help us to redeem and reconcile relationships by recognizing that an offense was made, and we show our consideration for the relationships in our lives when we show that we care enough to want to heal and restore them.

True becoming in a marriage requires a responsible look at the self and what we as individuals bring to the table, and being honest enough to recognize that some of the things we bring aren't the most appealing of behaviors. When we become more self-aware, we can work on understanding how what we do affects our spouse, and we can begin to make more considerate decisions in the process. Self-awareness helps our relationship become better because we are more conscious of what we can do to each other through our actions.

Questions to Discuss Together

1. Look at the session the pastor had with Lynn and Derrick. Do you see yourselves repeating any of their behaviors? If so, what might help to show the other you respect her or him?
2. It is difficult to love others if we don't love ourselves. Do you love yourself? Tell your partner what you love about yourself.
3. Tell about a time each of you has forgiven the other person. After telling the incident, both of you tell how you felt once forgiveness was given.

Action Step

Individually, work on the list of six ways to help you become self-aware. If it is helpful, talk with a friend about this step.

NOTES

7

Becoming Mature

Taking Responsibility for Our Deeds and Actions

A single bracelet does not jingle.

—Congolese Proverb

When I was a child, I talked like a child, I thought like a child,
I reasoned like a child. When I became a man, I put the ways
of childhood behind me.

—1 Corinthians 13:11

Maturity and self-awareness are incredibly close relatives. To be
self-aware means you possess some level of maturity. For our
purposes, however, self-awareness is the *process* of understanding
who you are, and maturity is the *act* of being responsible for who
you are. We often look at maturity when it comes to marriage
as someone who can contribute to the household bills, who can
help with the chores around the house, and who can keep some
level of income coming into the household. All of these things
do require some level of maturity, but when we dig deeper into a
healthy relationship, the truth is we need to get a little bit more
than that from a mature individual. In fact, maturity is one of
the essential *becoming* qualities, because it helps the other qualities emerge and display themselves in an effective manner.

Maturity is understood as having or showing the mental and emotional qualities of an adult. A person is considered mature when he can function like an adult functions.
We again attribute the evidence of maturity as one who can
perform certain practical responsibilities, but the definition of
maturity also looks at the mental and emotional qualities of an
individual. Here is where we can run into some challenges in

our relationships because we might execute a practical behavior without any hesitation but fall short on demonstrating our emotional maturity. We confuse the task of acting out a behavior or duty with the maturity of marriage, and we often don't show a level of maturity to our partners at all.

Maturity in a relationship recognizes that things might not proceed as we initially planned, but we can still grow and develop a healthy marriage with a deliberate effort to see the bigger picture of a successful marriage. Unfortunately, in some newlywed couples, each tries to force fit their spouse into the idea of what they want and expect them to be. Many social messages tell us that marriage is about having someone cater to your every whim and fulfill all of your heart's desires. When we define love in those terms, we see love as what someone will do for us, or how someone will take care of us, meaning that we are looking for someone to overcompensate for emotional things that didn't take place in our lives prior to this relationship, and we find ourselves working not on our marriages, but working on our spouses to have them conform to the idea and image that we created in our mind —in reality, those things that we are drawn to can become a point of contention later on. All of us in relationships can name traits that we used to appreciate or even admire about our spouses but that now wear us out and sometimes even get on our nerves. Mature people in relationships understand that they don't hang their entire success of their marriage on habits and quirky behaviors, because they will change in a marriage, and, the truth is, we have our quirks as well.

Julie and Danny have been married for almost a year, and they made an appointment to see me to get some clarity on some issues in their relationship. When they arrived, Danny appeared flustered, yet Julie was as calm as a cucumber.

> **Pastor:** How can I help you good people? Why are we here today?
>
> **Danny:** Pastor, do I have to do everything she says?
>
> **Pastor:** What do you mean?

Danny: Julie says I'm supposed to provide for her and take care of her, and I do, but she says I don't understand what married life is about because I'm not connecting with her.

Pastor: Julie, do you think Danny is supposed to do everything you say?

Julie: Well, not when you put it like that. I mean I don't expect him to be a slave or anything, but I do expect certain things and a certain level of treatment.

Pastor: What kind of things do you expect?

Julie: Well, I expect him to call me to see if I'm doing all right during the day. I think he should come home right after work to see if there is anything we need to do before he makes plans, and I expect him to make time for me so that we can go somewhere at least once a month.

Pastor: Julie, what happens when Danny doesn't meet those expectations?

Before Julie can answer, Danny cuts in.

Danny: *Happy wife, happy life*, that's all she says. When I make plans or don't do what she thinks I should do, she tells me I don't care about her, and that's not true at all. I love Julie very much, but she doesn't think I care unless I'm doing what she wants me to do, and I try because I want her to be happy. All day when she wants me to do something she ends it with *happy wife, happy life*, but I don't mind telling you pastor, I'm not too happy.

It is clear that Danny and Julie have some work to do within their marriage, and theirs is one example of how communication problems can occur in a relationship. Julie and Danny have to talk about how each understands affection and loyalty. Julie can't control Danny into being a good husband, but she does not seem to understand that. At the same time, Danny needs to hear and understand why she reacts the way she does. How Julie and Danny work through this experience can be the difference between understanding marriage as a contract or a covenant.

A contract is a rigid partnership that is based on checklists and strict obligation. A covenant relationship is one that is based on the connection of the two individuals and recognizing that the relationship works under the spirit of God's love. When you look at marriage as a contract, you see it as a list of things one should do, and if those things aren't done, the contract has not been honored. When you understand marriage from the perspective of a covenant, you still understand that there are certain obligations in the relationship, but you also recognize that at any point forgiveness may need to be extended. Marriages that operate as covenant relationships are the domain of the mature.

Mature people in relationships recognize it is not about the checklist of dos and don'ts but about the constant working with one another. Anyone who is guided by a "to do" checklist will ultimately not feel appreciated and could come to a place where the person feels used for only what he can do and not who he is. Mature love is loving each other despite our shortcomings. This is the type of marriage Danny and Julie want, but they must work to get there. Danny must come to understand that doing everything for someone is not love. He won't find true happiness if he believes his job is waiting to serve Julie's every desire in every moment. Love is about giving, but it is not about being a servant. To do things for a spouse is a nice thing, and even sweet in many situations, but you should not expect your spouse to wait on you hand and foot.

During the office visit with Julie and Danny, it was also discovered that he was raised in a single parent household and helped his mother raise his younger siblings. Because Danny was a child sometimes operating in a parent role, the interpretation of what his role was in marriage got crossed. He would take instructions from his mother and operate as an adult, so when he got married, he continued the same practice, coming to understand being helpful was doing everything a woman told you to do. Danny interpreted "happy wife, happy life" and operated in his relationship with his wife the same as he did in his relationship with his mother. In the process, he was cutting out his sense of worth, who he was as an individual, and what mattered to him in the relationship, and it was making him miserable. Maturity includes not just how you treat other people in a relationship, but it also includes how you should be treated, how you understand your sense of self-respect, and how you understand self-care.

IMMATURITY COMES AT A COST

When we examine the cost of immaturity with the help of the biblical text, we can see a great example of what doesn't work, through the life of Samson. Samson was a Nazirite, meaning that he was set apart by God to live a life that was worthy of service to the Lord. Samson had great strength, but one of his biggest challenges was his impulsiveness; he wanted what he wanted. But when it came to Samson's relationships, his need to have what he wanted got him in trouble.

Samson fell in love with a woman named Delilah, but their relationship was dysfunctional at best. It was fraught with their tricks, lies, and deceit, yet they remained together. The Philistines had a plan to destroy Samson, if they could pinpoint the source of his strength, and Delilah was used to help their cause. Much of Samson and Delilah's relationship was spent with her trying to locate his power. After Samson tricked Delilah three times about the root of his strength, Delilah asked him, "How can you say, 'I love you,' when you won't confide in me?" (Judg. 16:15). Between Delilah's manipulation and Samson's deceitful immaturity in understanding love within a relationship, he finally tells her his secret. Sampson's admission gets him in quite a predicament with the Philistines, and Samson loses his sight because, symbolically, he lost sight of who he was and he was not mature enough to handle this relationship.

Samson's story isn't unusual. Chasing what you want, without examining the consequences, happens all the time. You see what you want, or have an idea of what you want, and you have to have it no matter what. One of the problems is, when what you want doesn't turn out the way you thought it would, or you realize that what you wanted comes with great responsibility, you end up resenting and neglecting the thing—or person in your life. Maturity is understanding that relationships, like all things, require an investment. It is very rare that things will happen simply because that is what you want. If you want to have a healthy relationship, you must be willing to make an effort to take care of what you have. Marriage cannot be all about one person. You made a commitment to your partner, and this means you must consider their feelings, thoughts, attitudes, and perspectives. If your idea of marriage includes having someone take care of you, fix your problems, and adjust to your schedule, you will soon have a frustrated spouse, and you will likely be frustrated, too. The reality of mature love is not looking at what you will get but understanding your commitment to give. Everyone has ideas about what they think marriage will be, and there is nothing wrong with that. The mature person, however, recognizes among the "expected" ideas will come the unexpected. The true test of marriage is how to deal with the unexpected.

WHAT DID YOU EXPECT?

New couples often believe that marriage will make them happy. For a period of time, that may be true. Happiness in the early stages of marriage is about the possibilities that exist within the union. It is pleasant to speak about the future and the things that a couple can build together, but after the conversation is over and the hard work begins, the happiness seems to evaporate. Often you get disappointed when you realize that the person you married may not be the "key" to your happiness. Instinctively, you look to your mate to pick up where your parents left off. If parents did certain things or even if they didn't do certain things, so that we felt we were somehow cheated, we will expect our marriage relationship to fulfill those spaces. It is important to understand how maturity will help with understanding not only the role and reality of our spouse, but our role and our reality as well.

Mature people who are in relationships recognize the need to look at the big picture. They understand that, just like in life, everything will not go their way in their relationship. That healthy dialogue requires that they listen and, at some level, appreciate their spouse's perspective. Mature people in relationships understand that they cannot be judgmental or criticize and that they have to respect their partner's feelings. In essence, mature people understand that they are the stewards of their partner's emotions in the sense that they care for them, they help them to grow and develop in the best way possible, and they understand the possibility and potential in them to do the same for them.

BECOMING MORE MATURE

Becoming mature in our relationships, if we are not there already, can be a tricky thing. It is much easier to develop a sense of maturity before you commit yourself to a marriage relationship. However, with work and commitment you can begin to develop the habits of a mature individual who is married, and that can help strengthen your marriage bond. The main thing to understand about maturity is that it is a mindset. It will be difficult to act mature if you don't see the need for maturity in your relationship. A mature perspective will help you see things in a broader sense than how you already see them, and you can communicate more effectively with your spouse when you approach them with a different level of maturity. Here are some practical ways to operate more maturely in your relationship:

Consider your partner's feelings. Understand that your feelings aren't the only ones that matter. It would be irresponsible to assume that your spouse doesn't have any thoughts or feelings about anything you discuss. Take serious consideration for the fact that they have opinions and thoughts about issues as well. The things you talk about aren't only important to you; if your spouse has an opinion, it is important to them as well.

Know how to talk to your spouse. When you talk with your spouse, be careful that you are not judgmental. Make sure that when you find yourself in conflict, you are not trying to do damage to a person emotionally. Find ways to get your point across as reasonably as possible. Try to work on eliminating temper tantrums, because no one wants to be married to an infant. For more on the importance of good communication, see chapter 8.

Learn how to compromise. The world we live in is full of compromise—our relationship should be no different. Be open to listening to what your spouse has to say, and see if there is room for common ground. Sometimes there will be, sometimes there won't be, but that doesn't mean that you should never make an effort. Don't paint the living room green if your spouse hates green. Just because it works for you doesn't mean it will work for her. Don't minimize your spouse by telling yourself, "He'll get over it"—you would be surprised by how much people hold on to.

Want what's best for the relationship. What we often fight for is what is best for us, but what is best for us is not always what is best for the relationship. What we want is often about perspective and what makes us comfortable, when what might be best for the relationship might require that we stretch ourselves a little. Learn how to see different sides to a story, learn the benefits of having options. Most of all, always work to see what will be the best contribution to the health of your relationship.

Let your spouse be your spouse. Don't look for your spouse to be the mom who took care of you or the father you've always wanted. That is not the job description your spouse signed on for. Let your spouse operate as your partner, and try to grow as a couple. Trying to get your spouse to be your parent will simply keep you from growing and eventually have your spouse resent the role. Let your spouse help you to create a new story line.

Maturity is an asset to work with in every aspect of life, but it is especially necessary for a marriage relationship. Take time to evaluate your responsibility to one another as a couple, and always work to see the bigger picture. Understand the importance of being honest with yourself and being honest with your spouse. Recognize what you bring to the marriage table, and be responsible for it. Continue to look past your expectations and perceptions and continue to explore the new visions and directions you will create with your partner. Understand and respect the divinity of your partner and always see them through the lens of God's creation. The marriage journey might have seemed exciting as you came to the relationship, with your ideas and expectations of what the marriage would be like, but the lives of couples can become so much more exciting when we create new expectations with the ones we've commited to.

Questions to Discuss Together

1. Looking at the conversation between Julie and Danny, what happens when one spouse does everything the other wants and pays no attention to their own needs? How can you avoid that?
2. Looking at the difference between a contract and a covenant, what are each of you doing to make your marriage a covenant?
3. Go over the list of five ways to operate more maturely in your relationship and discuss which are easy for you as a couple and which are difficult.

Action Step

After discussing question 3 above, take some time individually and list strengths and weaknesses you have regarding the list. What are some things you want to work on? Come back together and discuss a few things you each want to improve.

NOTES

8

Becoming Flexible and Becoming Communicators

Learning How We Connect

▚▚▚▚▚▚▚▚▚▚▚▚▚▚▚▚▚▚▚▚▚▚▚▚▚

Talking with one another is loving one another.
—Kenyan Proverb

Know this, my beloved brothers: let every person be quick to hear, slow to speak, slow to anger.
—James 1:19 (ESV)

▚▚▚▚▚▚▚▚▚▚▚▚▚▚▚▚▚▚▚▚▚▚▚▚▚

One thing that will help you and your beloved as you "become married" is flexibility. The ability to adapt to your surroundings and make adjustments to plans, ideas, and expectations is vital. Flexibility in your marriage promotes the understanding that there is always another possibility to be considered. It also helps you, as a couple and as individuals, recognize that change is possible at any given moment. Often in relationships you have plans and ideas, as individuals and as a couple. When plans have to be adjusted, stress can be introduced into an otherwise healthy relationship.

Flexibility is often difficult because many are reluctant to change. Change can be uncomfortable and troublesome. Change is also something you often want someone else to do; it can be unsettling to think of yourself as a person who needs adjustments.

We struggle with flexibility early in our relationships because we are confronted with what I call the D.A.R.E. moments in our marriage. D.A.R.E. stands for Discoveries, Awakenings, Revelations, and Enlightenments. The different things you D.A.R.E. to find out can make your transition into marriage difficult. The important thing to remember is to have your own D.A.R.E. list—it is not about who wins the stalemate but who is willing to operate out of a sense of mutual benefit for the good of the relationship. Flexibility is connected to both qualities of self-awareness and maturity, because you need both to display a level of flexibility in your relationship. The quality of flexibility mandates that you open yourself up to different opinions, ideas, and perspectives. Flexibility means you are constantly working to be the kind of spouse that you would like to see in your partner.

Joe and Sarah are an older couple who found each other later in life and decided to marry. Both were married previously and had grown children. They had difficulty readjusting to married life.

> **Sarah:** Pastor, I need you to help Joe understand that his old fashioned ways aren't working anymore.
>
> **Pastor:** What do you mean?
>
> **Sarah:** Before I married Joe, I was doing everything myself. My husband passed away, and I had to work to support the children. I got to the place where I liked to work; I enjoyed making and having my own money. Now that we are married, Joe is upset that I am still working. He wants me to stop working because he thinks he should be the provider for us. I don't want to make him feel less than a man, but I don't feel I should have to give up my job just because I'm married.
>
> **Pastor:** Joe, Sarah seems to think that you don't want her to work when work is something she enjoys doing. Is she right in thinking this?
>
> **Joe:** It's not that I don't want her to do what makes her happy; it's not even that I don't want her to work. If I wasn't able to provide for us that

would be another story, but I make a good living, and she doesn't have to work because I'm supposed to take care of her—that's my job.

Pastor: If you don't want her to work, what would you like her to do with her time?

Joe: She can do some things, I mean like she can do things wives do. She can take care of the house and things like that. I mean basically I just want her to relax. She's worked hard for a long time. She's taken care of her children and raised them to take care of themselves; I just want her to enjoy relaxing and our time together.

Sarah: You don't want me working but what am I supposed to do when you're at work? All of that stuff is done whether I work or not. I take care of all the house things anyway. Did you ever think that I work because I enjoy it? You enjoy what you do, don't you?

Joe: Yes, but you were working then because you had to; when your husband passed you were the only adult in the house. But now you don't have to; I'm here to provide and take care of that stuff. We will have more than enough to live on.

Sarah: Pastor, I don't want more than enough; I want a job!

Sarah worked to support her family, but through her work she found a sense of independence and self-worth. In her second marriage, it is not money that she seeks but that sense of gratification and purpose she feels from a job. Joe's understanding of marriage is that Sarah doesn't need to work because there is enough money to have a good life. He does not understand why Sarah feels the way she does. Because Sarah started working when her first husband passed away, Joe assumed it was just a need she was meeting. He assumed she was working out of necessity, not self-fulfillment. Joe has to learn to be more flexible in his understanding of what is important to Sarah. Joe and Sarah are the perfect example that the differences, or commonalities, in age and experience do not automatically mean two people will share opinions.

BECOMING MORE FLEXIBLE

To become more flexible, you will find yourself running into some hard truths about yourself and your spouse. This does not, and really should not, be a negative experience. The key to understanding marriage is knowing that it is a constant learning process. Hitting a wall can be a great learning tool. A mature person is flexible because they recognize that things cannot continue in the same way and be healthy for the relationship. In a mature relationship, you learn how to compromise.

"Compromise is the act of working two ideas together to benefit all parties involved. Compromise is the art of negotiation. You are going to have to compromise in your marriage on a constant basis. Regrettably, compromise is not a word that is often used in marriage much anymore. Society teaches you to fight, or manipulate, your way to your goals. As a result, your relationship will begin to suffer. Thoughts of who is "in control" fill your thoughts and actions. You watch movies that "play the game" of getting the opposite sex to do what you want them to do, through tricks and self-interest. You listen to your friends, who tell you, "If I were you I would . . ." for hours on end. You remember mistakes from past relationships and make your spouse pay for those mistakes, to make sure that you don't get "played" again. The act of compromise can become forgotten in marriage when there is an overwhelming desire for control; however, the need for control can actually make connection with your partner more difficult.

Compromise is the way that all healthy relationships stay on track. Compromise becomes easier when you are ready to forgive your own imperfections and accept your partner's imperfections. When working toward compromise, you should be genuinely invested in listening to your spouse. The consideration of your spouse's perspective not only helps the process of compromise and flexibility, it also helps strengthen your relationship overall. Your spouse will feel like they are being heard and that their feelings are important to you.

You cannot be flexible when you are angry, impatient, or upset. When you work from those negative emotions you will either want to get to the end of a conversation and say something insensitive, or you will become emotional and simply want to make a point. You need to keep a positive perspective if you want to reach your goal of compromise and being more flexible.

Some ways that you can become more flexible are:

Understand you can make mistakes. Don't feel that you need to work constantly to prove to yourself and your spouse that you don't make any mistakes or that everything you do is perfect. Give yourself permission to make mistakes. All of us are human, and you will have a better marriage if you understand you're not going to get things right all the time. Even when you don't, you can still have a good outcome.

Recognize your spouse is not perfect. If you don't get things right all the time, then don't hold your spouse to the same unrealistic standard. Know that mistakes aren't deliberate reflections on your partner's love for you. People all need to learn, so give your spouse time to know the learning curve, and, even then, be gracious enough to understand that they will continue to make mistakes now and then.

Have a positive outlook on marriage issues. Flexibility requires that you look positively at issues before they even begin. Look at situations from a positive perspective so that things have a greater chance of a positive outcome. If you enter into issues with the thought that things are bad, then that is probably how things will end up.

Be patient. Flexibility requires time. Things will not always happen as fast or as simply as you want them to. Sometimes you may have to invest in certain things a little longer than you expected. What is simple to you may not be as simple to your spouse. It may take your partner a little longer to realize your point of view. There will be times when you have to help your partner understand where you're coming from.

Be willing to compromise. Do not look at things as going "your way" or see yourself working a situation to help your agenda. Legitimate compromise is about both parties being heard and respected. Take time to consider a suitable solution; that way, both people can feel like they were taken seriously about their points of view.

Relax. Don't get so caught up in your schedules, your ideas, your plans that you can't include your spouse in the process. One of the ways we can become inflexible is when we think that our plans aren't happening like we want them to. Flexibility in marriage helps us to know that we are not the only one in the room, and our spouses may have something to say about the way things go. Open yourself up to a different way of seeing things work out—it is not as bad as you think.

BECOMING COMMUNICATORS

Communication skills can determine whether a couple will become closer or move further apart, not just by the possibility of what is being said, but also based on what is not being said. Communication is an essential marriage quality, and it is significant, but it must relate to having a mature perspective on what the responsibility of communication is for a couple.

Communication is the skill of understanding *how* to talk to others, in this case, your spouse. Marriage communication is not a debate. There may be components of debate in marital communication, but it is not supposed to be a win/lose scenario. Communication in marriage is about getting to a place of understanding. There will be times when, as a couple, it does not matter what is being shared or how logical your point of view seems to you; you will not convince your spouse that your point of view is the right one. Communication in marriage is not devoid of impasses. There will be things that you will never agree on: how to discipline children, how to pay bills, how to clean a bathroom, what's the best route to get to your in-law's house. But winning the dialogue does not need to be the goal. The goal is understanding. Mature couples recognize that they did not get married to be right; they married so they can be relational.

Samantha and Nigel have been married for eight years, and their communication practice is deteriorating. They are trying to figure out why they cannot connect.

Samantha:	We used to talk about everything, but now it seems that he doesn't have much to say to me.
Pastor:	What is happening that you think he doesn't have much to say to you?
Samantha:	He just comes in from work and sits down on the couch, and he won't talk to me unless I ask him a question or ask him to do something. And then we always end up fighting. It's like I'm bothering him.
Pastor:	Nigel, what do you feel about what your wife's saying? Do you think you've kind of checked out when you hit the couch?
Nigel:	I feel that what I'm doing is getting ready for battle when I come in the house. I sometimes don't want to even go inside because I know as soon as I come in, she's going to start fussing at me.
Pastor:	What do you mean fussing?
Nigel:	I am just trying to relax from a long day, and Sam wants to start talking. She starts asking me to do this, and do that, she wants a light fixed, she wants the garbage taken out, she wants me to start looking at the pictures of the sofa she wants to buy. Geesh. Doc, I just

	got home, do you think I can have a moment to get myself together just for a minute?
Samantha:	If I did wait for you to do any of those things, it would take forever for you to do them. I'm just trying to make sure that things get done.
Nigel:	See Doc, you see that, you hear the fussing? You haven't been here ten minutes and she's yelling at me; it's like this all the time.
Samantha:	If I'm yelling it's because you don't listen to me, and I'm frustrated. When I'm yelling, it's the only time you talk to me!
Pastor:	Nigel, what do you talk about when you aren't talking about the things she wants you to do?
Samantha:	(laughing) He is very talkative when he wants to eat. I can hear from him then, or when he wants to have sex. He'll talk like crazy then.
Nigel:	(laughs)
Pastor:	It is good that you two can share a laugh, but Nigel, think about my question.
Nigel:	(laughs) I talk to Sam all the time. I ask for food and sex so much because those are the times she's not yelling at me.

It's not necessarily a bad thing that Nigel needs to get his head together and decompress from a long day at work, but he needs to communicate that to Samantha in a way that she doesn't feel like she's not important to him. Conversely, it doesn't have to be a problem for Samantha to want to connect with her husband after not seeing him all day long, but her success will be how she goes about communicating that desire and expressing that feeling to Nigel. Yelling and picking fights will not bring Nigel closer to her; it will make him retreat even more. What both want is not unreasonable, but how they articulate their desires to one another can begin to create barriers to connecting in their relationship. As they interpret things now, Samantha thinks Nigel doesn't care and Nigel thinks Samantha is attacking him. Neither of those ideas could be further from the truth, but because they are not communicating effectively, their perceptions were starting to become their reality.

THE POWER OF WORDS

Talking is not just what you say, but it is how you say it. A good attempt at communication can come to a complete stop when the wrong thing is mentioned. Someone who is trying to have a meaningful conversation can have everything go south quickly if someone gets the wrong idea about what is being expressed. Talking is not just about words; it is about sentiment. Saying that you apologize with meaning can have a completely different effect than when you apologize and don't mean it. Making sure that you are choosing your words correctly and not looking to win, but in all things looking to be relational, is crucial.

Talking is essential, but it is no more important than how you listen. Listening is crucial because that is where you connect with your spouse. When you are listening intently and deliberately, it signals to your spouse that you are paying attention, and they can often feel your sincerity. When you take the time and listen to your partner, you are letting them know *who* they are is important. When your spouse feels like you have their concern, through connection, whatever the discussion is about is likely to reach an acceptable conclusion.

HOW TO HAVE BETTER COMMUNICATION

To have effective communication, the first thing mature couples do is recognize that it begins with the individual. Good communication is focused on who you are as an individual and what kind of effort you make to effectively communicate through the challenges and perspectives that you bring to the table.

It is also important to recognize that communication is gender specific, meaning that men and women have somewhat different ways of communicating. Generally, men typically start a conversation when they see an inherent need. To a man, when there is something that needs to be talked about, that is usually when you hear from him. When it seems like men aren't talking, or they seem to be comatose in front of the television, it's not that they don't want to talk—the issue may be that when the basketball game is on and his favorite team is down in the championship series, in his world there might not be much to say if it's not about the championships.

Generally, women, on the other hand, talk more, because talking is a way of connection. A woman sees communication as being a way to be close. A woman will not only talk about the game that is on but will talk about the color of the coach's tie, why is there a need for a three-point line, why she thinks there is an unfair advantage for the taller people on the court, and she will wonder why grown men need cheerleaders on the sideline with skimpy outfits. Your wife's conversation really has nothing to do with the game, much to your disappointment, but it has everything to do with connecting with you. A woman typically wants to share the things in her life with you, and she automatically assumes that, because you love her, you want to do the same. With these different perspectives, it's important to know how to navigate through communication skills. Ways to communicate more effectively are:

Take time to listen carefully. When you are communicating with your spouse, don't have the conversation just to get it over with. Take your time to listen to what's being expressed and shared. The fact of the matter is, if you listen intently during the first conversation you can avoid having the conversation again, which will increase your stress level.

Give your partner the opportunity to express himself. When you are listening intently, don't try to anticipate what your spouse is going to say; wait patiently and let them say what they need to say. Cutting someone off or acting like you're rushing him to get to your point will only frustrate him and make him shut down.

Check your body language. This cannot be stressed enough. Be mindful of your facial expressions and your posture. Sitting with your back to your spouse while you're talking about something significant will frustrate her all the more. Rolling your eyes, holding your head in your hands, and twisting your face to look like a pretzel will not convince your partner that you are with her during the conversation

Don't try and fix things. This one is mostly for the men: Sometimes women just want to talk, they want to tell you about their situation and what happened with them, not so you can fix it but so they can feel connected to you. Coming up with the solution can frustrate wives because they can fix their problems, they just want you to sit tight and go along for the ride. Be attentive, be engaged in the discussion, but let them work it out.

Watch what you say. When I say watch what you say, I'm not talking about language, although that can be a part of it. I mean be careful with the words that you use. Be careful that you are not attacking or calling names. Make sure that you are not talking in a way that is demeaning or disrespectful. Remember the divinity in your spouse and respect it, as you would look for the same respect in return. A surefire way to kill communication is to make someone feel like she has been disrespected.

Say what you mean to say. When you are talking with your spouse, it is important that you say the things that need to be expressed. Don't limit yourself and think that you are keeping some things to yourself for the good of the relationship. If you don't say what you need to say, you will walk away feeling unsuccessful in your communication. You can eventually feel resentful and angry toward your spouse because you are holding things in. You can find ways to tell your spouse the truth about what you feel, even the difficult things, without being cruel. Being honest will help you both get to a better place in your relationships and your lives.

Communication is essential to the life of any relationship. When you take your time and become deliberate about how you express yourself with your communication, you can open the possibilities for sharing and caring in ways that you did not deem possible. Communication, when it goes well, can fuel a marriage or partnership.

Questions to Discuss Together

1. Being flexible means learning to compromise. Name a situation you have run into in your relationship where you have each shown a mature ability to compromise.
2. Read through the ways you can become more flexible. Which ones are easy for you? Which are difficult?
3. Would you say you are good at communicating with each other? Which of the communication skills listed are most important to you?

Action Step

Using the lists for flexibility and communication on pages 93–94 and 98–99, have each partner select five most important skills to practice in your relationship. Consider making a covenant of best practices you will both strive to follow as you become married.

NOTES

9

Becoming Better at Dealing with Conflict

Fighting the Good Fight

Tongue and teeth will meet.
—Jamaican Proverb

Do not let any unwholesome talk come out of your mouths, but only what is helpful for building others up according to their needs, that it may benefit those who listen.
—Ephesians 4:29

Conflict and arguments in a marriage are not the end of the world, nor are they a sign that your lives as you know it are over. These challenges simply mean that you two are individuals and have your own opinions and perspectives on things. Giving the issue of conflict its own chapter was not an accident but a focal point in the process and partnership of marriage. Having good communication skills is a good quality to have in marriage, but knowing how to resolve conflict is its own important quality as well. The issue is not that you fight but rather that you can learn to fight in a way that draws you closer as a married couple and not farther apart.

Particularly around the early stages of marriage, couples will have disagreements. When the disagreements begin to overshadow the agreements, marriage can begin to feel like one big argument. Couples can get frustrated because they begin to think that having conflicts means they are having problems, and that is not necessarily true.

Couples need to remember two things. First, arguing is not necessarily about the individual per se, meaning it's not the individual they are having an issue with, but couples need time to adjust to each other in their marriage. Sharing space, learning one another's habits and quirks, figuring out what strange habits your spouse has that you never experienced before, all of these things can stress a person out. When people are stressed they lash out, and when people lash out they are not always considerate and thus, conflict erupts. The second thing to remember is that many conflicts in the early stages in marriage can be resolved fairly simply with cooler heads. The issue is not the fact that you are fighting, but how you fight.

Certain language and personal attacks are triggers that will upset your spouse and make matters worse. You need to have boundaries, even in your disagreements, because there will be things that you cannot take back. And it is incredibly difficult to build a relationship back up from those moments.

Sharlene and Martin have been married for three years, and they are dealing with some fairly consistent conflict issues. They're not quite sure what to do next.

Martin:	You have to do something, Rev, because honestly, I don't think we're going to make it.
Pastor:	What seems to be the main issue?
Martin:	She doesn't know how to talk to me, and that just doesn't work for me anymore.
Pastor:	Tell me what she says to you.
Martin:	It's like she's ripping me apart for no reason. Whenever we don't agree, she calls me stupid. I don't like that; it's disrespectful.
Pastor:	Sharlene, is what Martin is saying true, and if so, why would you call him that?
Sharlene:	Because he says stupid things. I mean he's not "stupid," I mean I know that, but I just think he doesn't think things through.
Martin:	You mean I don't think the way you want me to think or do what you want me to do. Have you ever considered that how you talk to me

hurts my feelings? I mean, just because I don't say anything doesn't mean that it's OK to say those things.

Pastor: Martin, what do you say when she calls you names?

Martin: I don't say anything, because I'm trying not to start an argument. I mean, it's already bad, I'm just trying to stop the situation from getting worse.

Pastor: And how's that working out for you?

Martin: It's not.

Pastor: Sharlene, do you think it's nice or considerate of you to call Martin names? I mean, he seems pretty troubled by what you're saying.

Sharlene: I mean, I guess I can see how he might not like it, but Martin is different; he's relaxed and things don't bother him. That's not me. I like to make sure I get everything out in the open. I don't believe in holding anything back. That's how I was raised, to speak my mind.

Pastor: Well, speaking your mind is one thing, but calling someone names is something else. And even in speaking your mind, is Martin allowed to have his own opinion; I mean, can he speak his mind, too?

Sharlene: I guess. But I don't see the big deal. He's just so sensitive—I didn't know everything I say was going to be a problem.

Martin: Everything you say is only a problem because everything I do is a problem for you.

Martin and Sharlene clearly have a communication issue, but their issue turns into more of a conflict because of how they talk to each other. Clearly, they need to learn how to communicate with each other during moments of conflict. Sharlene does not seem to be too concerned with the fact that Martin is bothered by her sharp criticism. Something to consider: Sharlene grew up around a mother who had the same habits. Her mother always told her what she was not doing and what she needed to do. She grew up sensing that her mother was disappointed in her and was never satisfied. Without realizing it, Sharlene repeated her mother's behavior and criticized everything that Martin did. Sharlene understood this type of response as what was done to someone you cared about; thus, she never saw a problem with it. Martin would not, or could not, articulate his dissatisfaction with Sharlene's behavior, so it continued. Martin needed to learn that burying his feelings to avoid an argument or a stressful conversation did not produce happiness. If he was going to be a full partner in his marriage, he was going to have to speak up and make his needs and feelings known as well.

WHAT'S THE BOTTOM LINE?

In a marriage, an argument can take place over anything. Some think people fight over things that are major and life changing, but many couples can attest to at least one fight over driving directions, what they will eat for dinner, or the cap on the toothpaste. Some of the biggest blowouts in marriage can be over the smallest of things. That is because sometimes the topic of the argument isn't the issue. It is necessary for couples to be clear about the source of any conflict that arises. When the real issue isn't dealt with, no one is satisfied with the outcome of the conversation.

In Matthew 18:15, Jesus discusses the steps to dealing with conflict in relationships. He says, "If your brother sins against you, go and show him his fault, just between the two of you. If he listens to you, you have won your brother over." Although it is not a direct reference to marriage, Jesus provides the model for resolving conflict within marriage. The use of the word sin in the Greek is *hamartia,* which means to miss the mark, like an archer missing their target. In your marriage relationship, there will be times when you "miss the mark." You can miss the mark intentionally or unintentionally, and when you miss connecting with your spouse, it can hurt tremendously. The good news, however, is that Jesus reminds you that you can go to your beloved and let them know how his actions have affected you. The concept and principle of love used here is based on the understanding that if your spouse cares for you, she will take into consideration the feelings you have expressed. Jesus stresses that this sharing of feelings is between the two of you; it is not a moment of public display or spectacle for all to see. This is not a moment to embarrass or impose some kind of manipulation tactic to exploit the other. In fact, Jesus is trying to state that the one who is offended should be caring and considerate to the one who has made the offense. The fact that your spouse has missed the mark in connecting with you doesn't give you license to be offensive or hurtful to him, because that will create further fracture in the relationship. Care and concern needs to be shown between both persons so that the spirit of reconciliation can be established. The hope is that the consideration and love that comes from your partner will consider your feelings, acknowledge the wrong, and see a place of forgiveness. Then you can both grow from the experience.

The goal of every conflict in marriage is to grow the marriage, meaning that the end result should be to make sure that the solution that is reached will be the best for the relationship. When a couple realizes that their goal is the relationship, then they can move to a greater understanding of the issue. If the issue is simply the fact that you aren't getting your way, then you might be compelled to examine your motives and look to step out of your feelings and work to do what is good for the relationship. A large part of becoming a couple in marriage is understanding that we have to make room for a larger definition of what we believe marriage to be, and understanding the goal of resolving conflict is a helpful tool to carry with us throughout all aspects of our marriage.

HOW TO BECOME BETTER
AT RESOLVING CONFLICT

Resolving conflict in a marriage does not need to be difficult, but it does need to be deliberate. The first step is recognizing that you married someone else. This means that as much as you say you have married your soul mate, or your best friend, or your kindred spirit, you did not marry you. Your spouse will continue to have opinions and ideas that are different from yours, and that will continue for the rest of your marriage. Disagreements will occur, but if they are dealt with in a healthy manner, they can be good for the relationship. Different perspectives can open a door to many more possibilities than what you could produce on your own.

Couples also need to learn that as they share together, there are some things that they can grow into, and they can grow out of others. One of the things we can grow into is how we criticize the way our spouses do things. We need to realize that our spouses have their own way of doing things and that doesn't make them bad people. Some of the ways you can directly deal with conflict in marriage include:

Practice your approach. Be responsible for how you say what you say. Keep in mind your spouse's feelings, and make sure that you are considerate of what is important to them.

Be responsible for your own buttons. Know what sensitive issues are yours. When things come up that make you uneasy, don't blame your spouse. She isn't making you feel that way; you have to take ownership of the things that get you worked up.

Be honest about what you feel. Tell the truth about how things hurt you. You have full permission to talk about what you like and what you don't like, and you should be willing to discuss them openly.

Understand the goal. Know that you aren't in conflict to win arguments, but you are in this conflict to learn how your relationship can get stronger. Use every opportunity to see how you can grow from the mistakes and the marks that you have missed as a spouse.

Apologize. Don't be afraid to be the bigger person and admit when you have done wrong. Take ownership of your actions and what you do. Never put off apologizing when you know it should be done.

Use "I" statements. Instead of universal statements that don't take a sense of ownership, say how you feel. For example: "I feel exposed and embarrassed when you make fun of my clothes in front of your friends." Not, "You never consider my feelings when your friends are around." Your spouse can't win with a "You don't ever" statement. Talk about how you feel, putting your thoughts and feelings into statements that begin with "I"; that way, you can always leave room for connection.

Be ready to forgive. The truth of the matter is your spouse is not the only one who needs it. Forgiveness is the most significant healing tool of a marriage.

Take a break. Everything doesn't need to be worked out right away. If you find yourselves at a place where nothing is getting accomplished or emotions are too high, take a break, deal with it tomorrow, next week, or next month, but be willing to step back to refresh yourselves and calm down.

When you work through the conflicts of your marriage in healthy, productive ways, you can become closer because of the experience. Once you deal with the emotions and own your feelings, the lines of communication can become strengthened and honest discussion happens. It is the honesty of conflict that can be a true blessing to a relationship if it is done in a healthy, caring, and spirit-filled way that brings you two together instead of one conquering the other.

Questions to Discuss Together

1. Talk about a recent conflict where you both feel you dealt with it constructively. What did each of you do that helped the other feel heard and understood?

2. Talk about a conflict you had where one or both of you felt awful after the discussion. Why did you feel so

bad? In hindsight, what did you learn about each other's behavior, and how can you improve in the future?
3. Talk about how your family dealt with conflict. What behavior do you want to never repeat? What behavior do you hope to retain?

Action Step

Each of you make a list of two to three things that you know you say that will get under your partner's skin when you want to be hurtful. Perhaps you compare your spouse to a disliked parent. Then, make a list of two to three things your partner knows to say that get under your skin during a conflict. Share your lists with one another and agree to not use them in the future when conflict erupts.

NOTES

10

Becoming More Forgiving

Letting Go for the Good

If there is cause to hate someone, the cause to love has just begun.
—Wolof Proverb

Bear with each other and forgive one another if any of you has a grievance against someone. Forgive as the Lord forgave you.
—Colossians 3:13

No healthy relationship can exist without forgiveness. Forgiveness is the process where you stop feeling anger toward another for what they have done and make the intentional, self-empowered decision to move past an issue with a person who is close to you. Throughout your relationship, you will have to extend forgiveness to your partner. Forgiveness is a "becoming" quality in marriage because it requires that you acknowledge that some things will need to be let go of so that the relationship can continue to grow.

In a marriage, forgiveness means you do not allow the wounds from your past to influence and control your life. When you forgive, you are making the decision that ultimately the past will not predict the future. Forgiveness means that you operate from the place of possibility and potential. When you forgive, it is a signal that you still believe in the possibility of the relationship. When you forgive, you are declaring that you are invested in the commitment that was made. Let's be clear. Forgiveness is not the act of taking whatever is done in the relationship and going along with it. For example, violence toward one spouse is not something to simply forgive and forget.

Forgiveness is difficult for many couples because they don't see many examples of couples working through difficult situations. Soap operas, television shows, and romance movies can have an "if it doesn't work move on" type of approach. You take commitment with a grain of salt when the characters on the soap operas marry, divorce, and then marry another, all before the first commercial break. You may enjoy the programming but not take the time to consider the psychological impact that it has on you when it comes to real-life relationships.

Phil and Tracy have been married for twelve years, and both are wondering where the relationship is headed. They are trying to figure out how to move their relationship forward.

Phil: I'm not sure that Tracy cares about me anymore. I just feel like she has disconnected with me in some way.

Pastor: What has brought these feelings on?

Phil: I don't know. I know she cares about me, but I don't think she loves me. I don't know if that makes sense, that's just what I feel.

Tracy: He knows why I have pulled away; he just doesn't want to say anything to you about it.

Pastor: Phil, do you know what Tracy is talking about when she says you know why she's pulling away from you?

Tracy: He told me that he would rather not be married to me because it was too much of a burden to be married to someone who had so many "issues." I feel if he feels like that, then why does he even bother dealing with me?

Phil: I explained that to you already. I told you what I meant by that was that if the relationship was going to stay like this, with us fighting all the time, I could really do without it. We didn't need to be married if all we were going to do was fight. Besides, that was like five months ago—you are still angry with me over that?

Pastor: Tracy, Phil's words must have seriously disturbed you and must have really struck a sensitive spot somewhere. Why do you think his words hurt you like that?

Tracy: Well, I feel if he thinks that I am too much of a problem or too much to handle, then why stick around; I mean it's not like you haven't tried.

Pastor: Have you really tried? I mean, it seems that it might be kind of difficult to work on a relationship when you are holding on to something that was said five months ago.

Tracy: Well, his words were serious, and he's acting like it is no big deal now. But when he said it he was fired up and yelling and then walked out.

Pastor: Phil, do you want to leave? Do you want to end this relationship?

Phil: No! I want it to work; I don't want it to be over. I just think things can be harder to do if some adjustments aren't made.

Pastor: Tracy, what do you think about that?

Tracy: You can talk about it, but the reality is he said what he said. I don't know what he can do to change that, and I don't know if I can trust him or believe that he's serious about being together after his announcement to me and the world.

It is obvious that Tracy and Phil have some serious decisions to make, but one of the most immediate issues they must figure out is how to move from a place of hurt so that they can have a real conversation about their feelings and what they will do with their relationship. Phil needs to make sure that he chooses his words more wisely, even if he finds himself in places where his emotions are getting the best of him. This is one of those instances where words have hurt, and he is going to have to work hard at repairing the breach that was created. Tracy will have to decide whether or not she is going to forgive the statement that Phil made so that the relationship can begin to heal and move forward. For some people reading this book, Tracy's anger may seem like a small thing, but you might be surprised at some of the things your spouse holds on to when they are in pain. In Phil's mind, the incident was over and done with almost immediately after it happened, especially after the apology was made. But for Tracy, her concern is not so much what was said but the sentiment behind it. It's not that she did not hear Phil's apology; it is clear she did. But she is going to have to move on from the place of the apology and move forward if she wants to continue to grow the relationship with her husband.

WHY CAN IT BE SO HARD TO FORGIVE?

In Matthew 18:21, Peter asks Jesus how many times he should forgive someone. Peter thinks that surely there has to be a limit to the times that you can look past what someone has done to you. Peter, trying to be as rational as possible, throws out what he believes is a decent number and says, "'Up to seven times?'" Jesus, always encouraging his disciples to see the bigger picture, tells him, "'I tell you, not seven times, but seventy-seven times.'" Some translations indicate the number Jesus gave was much larger, but that is not the point. Jesus isn't telling Peter to keep score. In fact, he's telling him the exact opposite. Jesus is saying whether the number was seventy-seven times, four hundred and ninety times, or three thousand times, it should be a number that is too difficult to keep score. When you are keeping score of the offenses that are done to you by your spouse, you are paying more attention to building an argument of what is wrong with them or perhaps why you shouldn't be with them, and you are less focused on growing and building a relationship with them.

Simply put, infractions are distractions, and when you focus on keeping score, you will have little time to talk about the important things that make a relationship strong. There are two reasons Jesus attributes such a seemingly random number to acts of forgiveness: (1) He wants you to feel silly for trying to keep count; and (2) He wants you to learn that keeping a record of wrongs in the first place is the real act that needs to be forgiven. When you think of the forgiveness you receive from God's grace each day, you don't have enough character collateral invested in holding someone else to any specific standard. In marriage, the act of forgiveness and grace go hand in hand.

HOW TO BECOME MORE FORGIVING

The process of forgiveness is one that begins and starts with the individual. What often happens is we look at forgiveness through the lens of emotion because of the wrong or the rule that was broken, but forgiveness is about making a conscious decision to process and think through the emotions for the good of the marriage relationship. Some of the things that can help us demonstrate the quality of forgiveness in our marriages are:

Identify your feelings about what happened. You need to be more specific about what you feel other than simply saying, "You hurt me." You need to express clearly your feelings about what was done or said so that you can articulate that to your spouse.

Take ownership for what you feel. Understand what rules you have that have resulted in your feelings. Be honest about where they come from, be it past experiences or some similar instance that you have not been able to let go of. Be mature enough to understand its origins.

Give your spouse an opportunity to explain her perspective. It doesn't matter what happened; as long as there is more than

one person involved, there is going to be another way of looking at the situation. Give your spouse the respect to hear where
they are coming from and how they see the situation. You can
have your mind made up of how you feel, but you need to be
open about why the action took place.

Forgive yourself. If you are finding it difficult to forgive your
spouse, you might want to look at who you are actually holding a grudge against. It might be a parent, someone from a past
relationship, a former or current co-worker or boss; once you
can pinpoint the issue, give yourself the permission to let it go
so that you can live in the now.

Don't use a big paintbrush. People make mistakes, but they
are not the mistakes they make. We all commit infractions and
slip up throughout our lives. Don't make someone else's mistakes larger than yours. If you can recognize that you will make
mistakes from time to time, don't look for perfection from
your spouse. It's unrealistic and unfair.

Don't use past hurts as weapons. Don't use what has happened to you as a credit card that you can pull out to use for
emotional collateral. If you keep bringing up an issue, you are
not over it. If you are not over it, you need to find a way to get
over it and move on.

Learn how to accept an apology. People can be genuinely
sorry for what they have done. Learn that people can grow
from the mistakes they make, and relationships can be stronger
when couples work through moments of forgiveness. Look at
being an agent of grace in your relationship, and extend your
personal spirit of love.

Talk about new patterns of behavior. Have some dialogue
about how to avoid the same offenses in the future. Make a
covenant to both agree on what each of you will do to avoid
a similar situation in the future. There may have to be some
mutual compromise. Be open to the fact that both parties may
have to change their behavior as you move forward.

When you operate with the quality of forgiveness in your
relationship, you allow the possibilities of new pathways in
your marriage to develop. Forgiveness helps you not only learn

from the experience, but it can help you to learn to love in a deeper way. Through forgiveness, you can better understand what partnership means and what is really important in the process of developing a lifelong connection. Forgiveness is the act of looking at the bigger picture and declaring to each other that your commitment to work things out is greater than the hurts that you will experience.

Questions to Discuss Together

1. In your relationship, what is something for which you need to be forgiven? Have you asked for forgiveness? What happened?
2. According to a popular saying, we tend to judge ourselves by our intentions, but we judge others by their actions. How do you understand that? Is it fair? Do you do this?
3. What do you need to forgive in your relationship? Has forgiveness been sought? What should you do if you feel hurt and the person doesn't ask you for forgiveness?

Action Step

Practice forgiveness. Each of you think of something you need to ask forgiveness of from the other. It may be something very small. Apologize to the other person during this week, and talk about how it felt for both of you.

NOTES

11

Becoming Sexual

Unlocking the Intimate Purpose of Marriage

▚▚▚▚▚▚▚▚▚▚▚▚▚▚▚▚▚▚▚▚▚▚▚▚▚▚

Coffee and love taste best when hot!
—Ethiopian Proverb

This is my lover, this is my friend, O daughters of Jerusalem.
—Song of Songs 5:16b

▚▚▚▚▚▚▚▚▚▚▚▚▚▚▚▚▚▚▚▚▚▚▚▚▚▚

It has been said that when sex is good it is only 10 percent of
what matters in a marriage, but when sex is bad it is 90 percent
of what matters in a marriage. Sex and intimacy play a significant part in the marriage relationship, and you don't need to
act like it is not a factor. The expression of love through the
physical intimacy of sex can be a large part of the marriage connection. Marriage is about sharing, and one of the ways that
you share with each other is through the act of sexual intimacy.
When you talk about sharing with each other as partners, you
have to understand that the giving of the self also includes
intimacy. Sexual intimacy is the proverbial icing on the cake
when it comes to relationships. If a couple is physically able to
participate in sexual activity but for whatever reason does not,
it can be an indication of some greater issues of sharing and
intimate connection.

This chapter explores sex as a larger manifestation of intimacy. Sex is not the only way in which a couple can be intimate, but you should understand the importance of sexual
expression. As much of the focus in this book has been for
couples to become married, the same sense of becoming must

take place in your sexual connection. It is no secret that many couples, including Christian couples, have shared in sexual intimacy before marriage, so the assumption is that couples feel they have the sex portion of the relationship covered. While there may be some level of sexual compatibility, there is still a responsibility to your partner to understand not only your partner sexually but also yourself.

For many years, sex has been looked at in the lens of the Christian faith as a necessary evil. Sex was in many cases looked at as a vile and unpleasant occurrence because it was considered a physical act, and everything that was not dealing with the spirit was considered flesh, and flesh was negative. To operate with a desire that arises from the flesh was frowned on. As a result, the approach and perspective of sex for those from the Western Hemisphere is one of a more conservative and strictly Puritan modality. Even now, many Christians in some more conservative circles see sex not as an expression of love, but rather as a Christian duty, meaning if you are not engaging in sexual activity for the procreation of the human race, then you are operating out of a sense of physical desire and hence are operating in the context of sin. Because of this approach to sexual behavior as well as sexual identity, many men and women have come to see sex as negative, dirty, and shameful. This is problematic, because as human beings we have natural, biological desires. This has created what can only be described as an unnatural paradox within the spirit of some people: Why is it that I feel these things and have these urges naturally in my body, and why am I being taught that it is bad to feel them? The issue of sex and sexuality has turned many individuals into repressed sexual beings who torture themselves with what their body is telling them and what religious society has instructed them to feel. As a result, many couples come into a marriage relationship either with a belief that sex is dirty and is simply a desire that needs to be shamefully fulfilled, or it is an act that is necessary only for making children and not for personal enjoyment.

When sex is looked at in this way, couples miss the opportunity to connect with each other in a deeper, more expressive manner. Sex is a mature act in the sense that it requires a responsible look at relationships as a whole, and with it comes the understanding of sex being the physical demonstration of a healthy relationship. When I was a teenager and adults were telling me to not have sex, it was usually connected to the risk of teen pregnancy or contracting sexually transmitted diseases (STDs). As I got older, I understood that the sexual act is such an intimate part of a mature relationship that it requires a more mature mind to deal with the responsibility of the physical sexual act. It is not that teenagers can't have sex. Statistics on teen pregnancy demonstrate that they can. What teenagers more than likely cannot handle is the mental side of sex, because it is that side of the sexual relationship for which they have not yet developed themselves or prepared. What I am saying is that sexual intimacy is more than a physical act, and the fact that your body can perform sexually does not mean that people are mature enough to receive or understand the meaning of sexual connection. There are adults who still do not understand sexual intimacy in healthy ways, and that is why many people are sexually repressed, sexually unfulfilled, sexually overexposed, and even sexually underdeveloped.

We bring all kinds of sexual understandings and ideas into the marriage relationship. Whether couples have an extensive sexual history before marriage or enter the marriage completely inexperienced, both spouses have some kind of idea of what to expect that sexual relationship to be and what it means as a couple. If you are reluctant to articulate your understanding of what sex means to you as an individual and how you interpret the sexual relationship in marriage to your partner, you will most likely experience an incomplete expression of your sexual desires and understanding that can lead to an unfulfilling sexual partnership. Some people fear sharing their desires because they do not want to be shamed for their feelings. As a result, they don't communicate, and their partner doesn't know what they want. Desires go unfulfilled.

As in every aspect of the marriage, communication is essential. Don't say you share everything with your spouse if you do not talk about sex and desire. Communication is a vital tool in all areas of marriage, including the expressions and sharing of sexual intimacy. Your focus in marriage, for you to enjoy a fulfilling sexual connection, should be to always have the space to express what you enjoy and understand about your sexual understanding and move toward working together to have a sexual harmony that satisfies both partners in the process.

When we speak of intimacy, we are speaking of a connection that takes place beyond the usual emotional connection of those we encounter. Couples that share a sense of intimacy are ultimately sharing a sensual, physical connection. Early in relationships, that sensuality consists of kisses, hugs, rubs, and caresses, which bring a sensation of closeness and connection that is mixed with the excitement of the courtship process. Couples begin to move to more sexual activity as time goes on, ultimately seeking a sense of connection. We value the sensual touch and displays of affection from our spouses. The closeness that comes with that connection moves us to express ourselves in more deliberate ways. For some, this can create a sense of anxiety. We feel inept or unprepared for sexual intimacy, and as a result, this can hinder the sexual connection.

Monte and Latrice have been married for two years and have experienced changes they do not understand in their sex life.

Monte:	We used to see each other and make things happen, you know, we would be all over each other. Now it seems like things have gotten . . . well, actually kind of boring.
Pastor:	That's kind of natural, I mean you will always be attracted to each other, but you won't always have that kind of energy; that doesn't have to be a problem. Latrice, what do you think about Monte's comments? Have things kind of slowed down between you two?
Latrice:	I don't think they have slowed down; I just think that things aren't the way Monte wants them.

Pastor: What do you mean? What do you think Monte wants?

Latrice: I'm not really comfortable talking about that kind of stuff with a preacher, it's personal stuff.

Pastor: Well, I understand it is a bit unusual, but I'm no stranger to personal stuff—preachers have sex too.

Latrice: Well, Monte wants to have sex all the time, in the morning, at night when you go to bed, in the shower, when you're in the living room watching TV, it feels like every time I turn around he's trying to have sex! I don't know if all of that is necessary.

Pastor: Is it the frequency or is it the locations where Monte's initiating sex that are bothering you?

Latrice: Umm, it's a little of each, I guess. I don't mind having sex; I just don't need to have it every day.

Pastor: Monte, Latrice says sex every day is a bit taxing; do you understand where she's coming from? What do you think about her take on the sexual frequency you share?

Monte: I don't know where this is coming from. I mean, it's not like I force myself on her. When we were dating, we talked about this, and she said she could have sex every day because she likes it. I didn't know I was causing a problem.

Latrice: I do like it; I enjoy having sex with you. It's just that now that we're married, every day seems a bit much. When you were talking about that back then, I didn't see you every day; you would visit and stay the weekend and then go back home, so sex for the weekend was no problem. But now, every day seems like too much.

Monte: OK, well why didn't you say anything?

Latrice: I didn't want you to think I wasn't interested anymore, and I was afraid that you would look for someone else.

Monte: I don't want anybody else. I just want you to be honest with me so I'm not making you unhappy and you start making me miserable.

Latrice and Monte are experiencing something that many couples face early in their marriages. Couples that have been intimate before they were married can mistakenly expect their sexual habits to stay the same, but the change of bringing two lives together will change sexual habits. Because of what they've been taught, some women agree to have sex with their boyfriends because they think it will keep their men happy and in the relationship. Some women have certain feelings about sex or sexual behaviors but don't share them because they want to be married and feel it is what is needed to obtain a man. When they finally get married, some women's sexual behaviors change because they don't see a need to keep up the same routines, much to the disappointment of their mates. This can create sexual frustration and feelings of resentment and misunderstanding.

GOOD BOYS AND GIRLS DON'T DO IT

Historically, the interpretations and understandings of sex are deeply rooted in the Greco-Roman philosophies that helped shape early Christian theology and, as a result, the dominant philosophy of the Western Hemisphere. Simply put, the philosophers had an either/or approach: the soul or the spirit was good, so then the body as a result had to be bad. The body was bad because it was the body that executed the bad deeds, violence was done with a fist, harsh words were spoken with a mouth, mean and malicious actions were done with a body. Consequently, anything that dealt with the flesh was considered evil. This of course translated into the world of sexuality all too easily. If the body did evil and negative things, then surely it would be easy to see sex as an offensive act. Christian theology continued this line of thought. The body, such as it is, is a finite, limited, borrowed house for the soul. Bodies are temporal and don't last long, but the soul is eternal, so therefore what you need to concentrate on if you truly want to be holy is developing the soul and not worrying too much about the body, especially in regard to sexual activity. In the book of Corinthians, Paul tells all who are not married and widows that it is better to remain unmarried, just as he was. Some scholars suggest this could either be linked to some type of persecution that Christians were facing in Corinth or the fact that Paul was placing his statement based on his anticipation of Christ returning in the immediate future. In any event, Paul minimizes the marriage relationship to ensure that Christians make their spirits a priority in terms of their salvation. As time went on, sex then functioned as a necessary evil because sex was needed to continue the human race. The sole purpose of the act of intercourse was to be faithful Christians and produce children as instructed, to "be fruitful and multiply." In fact, even now contraception is not endorsed by the Roman Catholic Church because using it does not produce children and would suggest that people are having sex for pure enjoyment.

One of the books of the Bible that is incredibly underrated is the Song of Songs, also known as the Song of Solomon. What makes this book so wonderful is that it is the discussion of two lovers who long to be with one another and who describe their sexual encounters with each other in a loving way. Christians have tried to make the book about the symbolic relationship between humanity and God. They have tried to make it about a committed couple grateful to God for their marriage. Some Christians say that the book is used as an allegory, meaning that its true purpose is to express God's love for the church. I have even heard it said that this is the story of two people who bring God into their bed with them to honor their Christian commitment. It is interesting that Song of Songs makes no reference to the Law or the covenant or Yahweh. It makes no attempt to explore the wisdoms of the faith like the book of Ecclesiastes or Proverbs. This book, with all of the Christian community's spin, is really only about one thing: sex! The sex that is explained in this book is beautiful, it is appreciated, it is reciprocated, and it is affirmed in the relationship between the two individuals. In Song of Songs, they celebrate the joy of experiencing kissing each other—chapter 1, verse 2—and the delight the man experiences in the form of his lover's breasts—chapter 4, verse 5—the sexual invitation to share as lovers—chapter 4, verse 16—and the joy of lying down and sharing themselves with one another—chapter 6, verses 2 and 3. The couple in this book makes no secret about how much they desire each other and see the physical need to be together.

HOW TO ENHANCE YOUR SEXUAL RELATIONSHIP

Sex is one of the few things that can be incredibly satisfying and in an instant become incredibly frustrating. Intentional work is required, and the need for understanding of where you are individually is essential. The good news is that if you are truly connected with your spouse, you have someone who is committed to working on this expression of love and affection with you, and the learning process can be a journey for the both of you. Ways to enhance your sexual relationships are:

Don't be afraid to talk. This cannot be overstated. Sex is a physical act, but sexual stimulation will happen so much easier if you aren't afraid to talk about your likes and dislikes. In fact, talking about things like what pleasures you and what fantasies you have can be quite stimulating to your partner.

Understand sex is meant to be enjoyed. Don't look at sex as some chore or obligation. Enjoy it. It's your body, and you have a right to have it feel good. If you are having trouble finding pleasure in sex, make sure you talk with your spouse and, if you need to, your doctor. There doesn't have to be anything wrong with you; you just might find some techniques that can help you.

Don't be afraid to try new things. After you've talked about your preferences and things you enjoy, find out where your common grounds are and begin to explore them together. Stay in communication with each other so that you can know what is and what is not working.

Make your spouse know you want her. This is also important in terms of communication. Sex isn't just had in the bed; pick up the phone and tell your spouse how desirable they are. Tell him how much you want him or how you appreciated the night before. Your spouse will be more involved in the process if she thinks she is desired by you. This isn't just for women. Men like to feel wanted too.

Be spontaneous. Call your spouse up and tell him to meet you at home for lunch. Tell her that you have just rented a hotel room for the evening for a nice night out, and she is the guest of honor. Let your spouse know that things don't have to be routine and that spontaneity adds to the spice.

Read books together. There are dozens of good books out there on sex for couples. Read them together and get ideas and talk about them. Don't be afraid to experiment and enjoy yourselves. It's fun to be frisky!

Enjoy yourself. Passion and sexual energy can be intense, but you don't need to look at lovemaking like work. Don't be afraid to relax and enjoy yourselves. Knowing how to laugh and be playful can reduce anxieties. Don't be afraid to laugh at yourself; sometimes things get funny. Have you seen yourself naked in a mirror lately?

Practice, Practice, Practice. If at first you don't succeed, try again. Lovemaking should be a special time of pleasure for couples. Make the focus about pleasing your partner, not about being happy with your performance. Continue to work on being the vessel of pleasure for your partner; once you become better at doing that, everything else will fall into place.

The gift of sex is one that can be rewarding as well as reinforcing to the marriage relationship. Once you learn who you are, in understanding your purpose for sharing intimacy, and come to know yourself in terms of your own sexual freedom and pleasure, you can open yourself up to a world of communication with your partner on an entirely different plane. The marriage relationship can continue to grow and expand, especially in the intimacy of physical expression, and God will show you how the physical connection can affect so many other aspects of your relationship.

Questions to Discuss Together

1. Name two or three messages you received from your family about sex, positive or negative.
2. Name two or three message you received from church.
3. How comfortable are you as a couple talking about sex? If you are not comfortable, what steps can you take to get more comfortable?
4. What do you hope you each will do when/if one or both of you are unsatisfied with the sex in the relationship?

Action Step

Spend some time together and create a mutual statement about the place of sex in your marriage and how you will communicate about it.

NOTES

Conclusion

Marriage is one of the most unique relationships in the world. Through the years, millions of couples have tried to better understand the path to marriage success. Many see misery as a requirement of marriage. Some use marriage as a vehicle for acceptance in society, regardless of the feelings or concerns of a spouse. Over time, marriage has morphed into a kind of high school on-again-off-again romance, with little to no concern for the welfare or feelings of those you have professed to love and cherish for as long as faith and love endure. Society suggests that if your marriage doesn't work, then, like automobiles, you are obligated to find another one. Your responsibility to your covenant relationship becomes shaky when things get too difficult, and the marriage does not turn out the way you expected. You might think that on some level you are doomed because the marriage you imagined will not become a reality. But the good news is there is hope for a happy union.

When you recognize that you are responsible for becoming the married couple that you want to be, you are forced to examine your role in the process. Your marriage may not be what you imagined, but in a real sense it can be better than you imagined; you just have to both be willing to work at it together. Understanding the journey of marriage begins with acknowledging that you are not in this journey alone. You have made a covenant to share your lives with someone who, for the most part, is being revealed right before your eyes. The beauty of marriage is also its hardest fact to face: that more and more with each day passing, you are learning more about your beloved, and you must realize that the only person you can change along this journey of holy matrimony is yourself. You have made a commitment to become something significant with your partner. You have entered a divine covenant: to talk through difficulties, to see your differences, to give of yourself, to examine yourself, and, most of all, to love your spouse through the lens of understanding what it means to love yourself.

The reality of becoming married is that there is no one formula. There is no magic pill except for the honesty that comes with knowing yourself and the love that is willing to discover what each new day will bring with your spouse.

The marriage process isn't done when the ceremony is over. No. After vows have been shared at the altar, and the "I dos" have been repeated and rings exchanged, and when all of the people have gone home and every gift and envelope has been opened, and the silence and reality of what happened starts to settle in, you will look across the room and see this person who has made the same commitment you have, that from this day forward, the commitment has begun to love, honor, and cherish, for better or for worse, for richer or for poorer, in sickness and in health. The real discovery unfolds. You are not only "just married" but you are on the journey of *becoming married*. Let the journey begin!

NOTES

Notes

Introduction

1. Brad Plumer, "These Ten Charts Show the Black-white Economic Gap Hasn't Budged in 50 Years," *Washington Post*, August 28, 2013, https://www.washingtonpost.com/news/wonk/wp/2013/08/28/these -seven-charts-show-the-black-white-economic-gap-hasnt-budged-in-50 -years/?utm_term=.83a1b5e47e4c.

Chapter 1: Becoming Aware

1. Anita Baker, vocal performance of "Fairy Tales," by Michael J. Powell, Vernon Fails, and Anita Baker, recorded 1990, on *Compositions*, Elektra, 33 1/3 rpm.

2. John Karter, *Introducing Psychology of Relationships: A Practical Guide* (London: Icon Books, 2012), 9.

3. David Livingstone Smith, *Why We Lie: The Evolutionary Roots of Deception and the Unconscious Mind* (New York: St. Martin's Press, 2004), 19.

Chapter 3: Becoming Honest

1. Edward P. Wimberly, *African American Pastoral Care and Counseling: The Politics of Oppression and Empowerment* (Cleveland, OH: Pilgrim Press, 2006), 43.

2. Ronald W. Richardson, *Family Ties that Bind: A Self-Help Guide to Change through Family of Origin Therapy*, 3rd ed. (Bellingham, WA: Self-Counsel Press, 2012), 38.

3. Ibid., p. 39.

Chapter 4: Becoming Conscious

1. John S. Mbiti, *African Religions and Philosophy* (Oxford: Heinemann, 1990), 133.
2. Ibid., 16.

Chapter 5: Becoming Mature

1. Les Parrott III and Leslie Parrott, *Saving Your Marriage Before It Starts: Seven Questions to Ask Before—and After—You Marry*, expanded ed. (Grand Rapids: Zondervan, 2015), 23.
2. Robin L. Smith, *Lies at the Altar: The Truth About Great Marriages* (New York: Hyperion, 2006), 38.
3. Timothy Keller, *The Meaning of Marriage: Facing the Complexities of Commitment with the Wisdom of God* (New York: Penguin Group (USA), 2011), 151.
4. Smith, *Lies at the Altar*, 26.
5. Henry Cloud and John Townsend, *How People Grow: What the Bible Reveals About Personal Growth* (Grand Rapids: Zondervan, 2001), 213.
6. Ibid., 228.

Chapter 6: Becoming Self-Aware

1. Na'im Akbar, *Know Thyself* (Tallahassee, FL: Mind Productions & Associates, 1999), 25.

Printed in the USA
CPSIA information can be obtained
at www.ICGtesting.com
LVHW080748031123
761774LV00009B/144

9 780664 262952